DISCIPLINE

The Canonical Buddhism of the Vinayapiṭaka

BUDDHIST TRADITION SERIES

Edited by
ALEX WAYMAN

VOLUME 26

DISCIPLINE

The Canonical Buddhism of the Vinayapiṭaka

JOHN CLIFFORD HOLT

MOTILAL BANARSIDASS PUBLISHERS
PRIVATE LIMITED • DELHI

First Edition: Delhi, 1981
Second Edition: Delhi, 1995
Reprint: Delhi, 1999

ISBN: 81-208-1051-1

Also available at:

MOTILAL BANARSIDASS

41 U.A. Bungalow Road, Jawahar Nagar, Delhi 110 007
8 Mahalaxmi Chamber, Warden Road, Mumbai 400 026
120 Royapettah High Road, Mylapore, Chennai 600 004
Sanas Plaza, 1302, Baji Rao Road, Pune 411 002
16 St. Mark's Road, Bangalore 560 001
8 Camac Street, Calcutta 700 017
Ashok Rajpath, Patna 800 004
Chowk, Varanasi 221 001

PUBLISHED BY NARENDRA PRAKASH JAIN FOR
MOTILAL BANARSIDASS PUBLISHERS PRIVATE LIMITED,
BUNGALOW ROAD, DELHI 110 007

FOREWORD BY SERIES EDITOR

The author, John Clifford Holt, in his Preface, has various suggestions for an expansion of his original work, here reprinted. It is to his credit that he is personally unable to revise the first edition. This is because we have the good fortune of the best effort of an intelligent, hard-working scholar. One time he wrote this fine work on the Buddhist Vinaya discipline. We can take it or leave it, but prefer to take it.

It is a pleasure to include Holt's work on the Vinaya Piṭaka in the Buddhist Tradition Series.

Delhi, ALEX WAYMAN

August, 1994

FOREWORD

The concerns of historians of religions and buddhologists overlap in a variety of important respects. Certainly no interpretation of the history or phenomenology of religion can claim real authority apart from a serious grappling with Buddhist experiences and expressions. It is equally true that no modern scholarly interpretation of Buddhist life can be considered truly adequate unless it takes into account the continuity and discontinuity between the Buddhist patterns and correlated patterns that have been identified in the general history of religions.

But despite the mutual need for intensive interaction between the history of religions and Buddhist studies, the two disciplines have remained remarkably isolated. Historians of religions have tended to shy away from a serious engagement with Buddhism—particularly in its early and Theravāda forms. They have tended to treat these early and more conservative Buddhist traditions either as religio-historical anomalies, or as mildly deviant forms of Upaniṣadic Hinduism. From their side, buddhologists have shown little interest in the kind of categories and interpretative language needed to carry forward serious systematic studies of man as *homo religiosus*. Some buddhologists have maintained that early and Theravāda Buddhism are essentially philosophical or ethical systems, and not really religious at all. Others—who have had a more adequate understanding of the religious dimensions of their data—have been so preoccupied with the primary work of translation and philological analysis that they have failed to pursue the kind and level of understanding that can effectively engage the work of historians of religions.

In recent years a number of younger scholars trained in the history of religions have taken up the task of bridging the gap between their own discipline and the field of Buddhist studies. The goal of these scholars (see, for example, William LaFleur's forthcoming book on Medieval Japanese Buddhism, Daniel Overmeyer's study of Chinese Buddhist sectarian movements, John Ross Carter's recent explanation of the Theravāda conception of *Dhamma*, and George Bond's forthcoming work on scriptural hermeneutics in the Theravāda tradition) is two-fold. These scholars use particular categories developed by phenomenologists and historians of religions to give direction to their study of Buddhist texts. When they pursue their philological research they take great care to identify the distinctive character and content of the Buddhist tradition under investigation. As they proceed with their work they use their buddhological insights to refine and enrich the interpretative categories with which they began.

John Holt's exploration of the religious dimensions of the *Vinaya* portion of the Theravâda Buddhist canon represents a significant advance in this new genre of religio-historical studies that engage Buddhist materials. Holt quite self-consciously selects a central religio-historical category to provide a focus for his interpretation. Taking his cue from Joachim Wach, Holt identifies discipline as a primary type of religious expression that cuts across the parochial boundaries of religious cultures and confessions. He has undertaken the task of interpreting the *Vinaya* text as an instance in which the phenomenon of discipline appears in one of its truly "classic" forms. Through his sensitive employment of this central category, as well as his typically religio-historical emphasis on the importance of myths and stories contained in the text, Holt is able to make both a buddhological and a religio-historical contribution. He is able to pursue the buddhological significance of the *Vinaya* far beyond the level reached by previous interpreters such as Horner, Pachow, and Prebish. At the same time he is able, through his careful and comprehensive analysis of the *Vinaya*, to refine and enrich the religio-historical category of discipline. As a result of Holt's work, historians of religions will now be able to recognize discipline as an interpretative category having equal status with other primary categories such as "devotion," "meditation," and the like.

It is our hope and expectation that more religio-historical studies of Indian and southeast Asian Buddhism will continue to appear (see, for example, Walter Randolph Kloetzli's *The Teaching of Light : Toward a Mahayanist Cosmology and It's Placement in Buddhist, Indian and Eastern Indian Perspectives*, soon to be published by Motilal Banarsidass). As the interaction between the history of religions and Buddhist studies continues, it should become an increasing source of new life and vitality for both.

University of Chicago — FRANK E. REYNOLDS

February 12, 1981

PREFACE TO THE SECOND EDITION

I am very grateful to all of those readers who responded to the first edition of *Discipline* and to Motilal Banarsidass for urging me to publish a second. I remain convinced that this very important dimension of Buddhism needs greater emphasis in most academic courses of study and certainly in most textbook overviews. I hope that the continued availability of this introductory study might contribute in a modest way to raising the profile of the *Vinaya* for a few interested and well-motivated students.

Over the past year and a half, I have tried to revise various sections of this book in an attempt to bring my interpretations and arguments into sharper focus and to draw out their implications. In each instance I was frustrated with the results of attempts to revise. My efforts seemed to lead me into the direction of issues that demanded a far more thorough treatment than this little volume could hold and yet remain essentially the same book. In this brief preface to the second edition, then, I want to indicate some of the directions I have wanted to pursue, directions that might be profitably pursued as a follow up to this study in the future (if not by me, then perhaps by other scholars or teachers).

It seems to me that the Buddhist monastic discipline described in great detail within the *Vinaya* corpus begs for comparisons with other religious forms of monasticism, especially the Jain in the Indian historical context as well as various orders of Christian monasticism in the West. What does the *Vinaya* corpus share in common with other monastic traditions that would allow us to understand discipline as a distinctive mode of being religious in comparison to other types of religiosity? So as not to understand discipline simply as an autonomous type of spirituality, a form of spiritual pursuit unrelated to others, it needs to be seen how discipline, as a mode of religiosity, complements or is congruent with other ways of being religious. In this book, I have emphasized how it is related to ethics, ritual and religious law, but discipline should also be understood in relation to devotion, faith and mysticism in Buddhism as well as in other religious traditions.

Second, the *Vinaya* should also be studied to better determine its great significance in the history of Buddhism. Not only was it so formative for determining a distinctive Buddhist identity vis a vis other religious traditions in the early phases of its Indian history, but it was also the venue and substance for a great many internal debates about what truly constitutes the path of the Buddha in the history of Theravāda tradition in Sri Lanka, Burma, Thailand, Cambodia and Laos. Arguments that eventually became indicative of schismatic sectarian pressures occurred not only at the Second Great Buddhist Council in ancient India (described in the third chapter of this book), but on many other occasions in Anuradhapura (Sri Lanka) from the first century B.C.E. through the seventh century C.E., as well as throughout the history of Buddhism in Burma from the eleventh century right up until the twentieth. In each instance, what was at stake was a formal understanding of what exactly it means to live according to which prescriptions are attributed to the Buddha. Issues of behavioral propriety and authority were hotly contested.

Third, the *Vinaya* needs to be closely studied to analyze the various attitudes it contains regarding the feminine, both in an abstract conceptual sense as well as more concretely in relation to how *bhikkhunis* were regarded in relation to *bhikkhus*. Very often, this issue is merely glossed over by pointing out that the Buddha declared that, in addition to the rules laid down for *bhikkhus*, eight more were to be followed by *bhikkhunis*, including the provision that they pursue their spiritual paths under the supervision of *bhikkhus*. In fact, there is a great deal of information about *bhikkhunis* that remains to be studied in the sections of the *Vinaya* that contain case histories illustrating how specific rules should be adjudicated. In that rich material, it can be seen in general that gender was, indeed, a critical issue, but nonetheless a condition or state ultimately to be transcended as one makes progress along the path. Preoccupation with gender, by male or female about male or female, is taken as evidence, on the whole, of a mind still fettered by desire and attachment.

Finally, the importance of *Vinaya* in the Mahāyāna traditions of China and Japan has still not been fully appreciated, let alone systematically studied, especially by Western scholars. I suspect that some of the parallels, for instance, discerned between Theravāda *vipāssana* meditation and Rinzai and Soto Zen might also be extended by studying how the disciplined mindset cultivated through an application of the *Vinaya* is at work in all of these monastic contexts, though refracted in differing ways. In particular I think that studies of Dogen (for Soto Zen) and Kukai (for Shingon) that focus on the foundations of their interpretations of monastic life would also raise the neglected profile of the *Vinaya*'s importance.

These, then, are some of the items on an agenda for *Vinaya* studies that, no doubt, would also include many others, including studies of *Vinaya* commentaries written by Theravāda Buddhist monks in many and varied historical and socio-cultural contexts. I hope that some of these issues and materials will be addressed by others in the academic community, and others in the Buddhist tradition, who understand that what Buddhists *do* is probably more important than what Buddhists *believe*, or that what the Buddha *did* was an affective expression of what he *taught*.

Bowdoin College,
Brunswick, Maine
July 10, 1994

JOHN CLIFFORD HOLT

PREFACE

Spiritual discipline is the *sine qua non* of monasticism. For the individual Buddhist *bhikkhu*, spiritual discipline means the nurturing of a mental awareness that leads to control of one's response to the phenomenal world of conditioned existence. As such, discipline is an indispensable means for the *bhikkhu* intent upon making progress toward the soteriological goal of *nibbāna*. The rules of discipline, as they have been preserved in the Pâli *Vinayapiṭaka*, also function as an expression of the Saṅgha's normative communal identity. They constitute the means by which the early community codified and reified orthopraxy in light of its understanding of orthodoxy. It is my essential thesis that Buddhist monastic discipline is most fully understood when considered as a purposive affective expression of the Buddha's *dhamma*.

This essay represents a rewritten version of my Ph.D. dissertation (University of Chicago, 1977). In preparing the manuscript for publication, I have added new discussions, eliminated others, and rendered some in less complex fashion. All of these changes were due to my own conscious effort to introduce the bases of Buddhist discipline to an audience wider than one composed of buddhologists and textual specialists. I am fully aware that much work remains to be done to provide a more comprehensive account, especially with regard to the importance of Vinaya commentaries. If this essay has tread the path of oversimplification, I accept responsibility.

I owe debts of great magnitude to a number of people at the University of Chicago who were of immense help to me in writing this book. Professor Frank Reynolds continuously offered critical suggestions. I am grateful for such a dedicated mentor. Dean Joseph Kitagawa provided incisive comments and patient tutoring during the formulative stages of the project and Professor Mircea Eliade read through the dissertation manuscript and gave his helpful response. I would also like to acknowledge the stimulation and encouragement I received from Professor Jonathan Z. Smith. I am fortunate to have worked with these individuals in the field of history of religions at the University of Chicago.

Thanks go to the American Council of Learned Societies and Bowdoin College for financially supporting this project. Finally, I would like to express my deepest appreciation to Barbara Sjogren Holt who has been a part of this work since its inception. This book is dedicated to her.

Brunswick, Maine JOHN CLIFFORD HOLT
December, 1980

CONTENTS

CONTENTS

Chapter One

INTRODUCTION

Discipline is the ethos of Buddhist monasticism : the trail head of the path of purity leading to *nibbāna* and the fiber of the community's soul, a means to salvation and the nucleus of communal identity.

Our knowledge of Gotama's strategy for salvation must be gleaned from the pages of sacred texts that are many generations removed from his life. As is the case with studies of early Christianity, scholars have sought to discover the original teachings of the master through a variety of historical/critical and textual methods of interpretation. And, as it is with the Christian Gospels, the primary sources at our disposal bear the markings of heavy-handed editors. Although some studies have proved to be highly provocative with regard to the original teachings of the Buddha,[1] in the final analysis we must reserve definitive judgment. For the present, we must be content with the knowledge that our reconstructions of the Buddha's formula for salvation are dependent upon the manner in which that formula was understood by the early Buddhist community and then preserved in their sacred texts. In short, the salvation blueprint provided within the early texts must be acknowledged as an organized revision of the founder's message.

1. I am referring to the reconstructions offered by Mrs. C. A. F. Rhys Davids in her *Sakya or Buddhist Origins* (London : Kegan Paul, Trench, Trübner and Co., 1931) and her *Buddhist Psychology* (London : George Bell and Sons, 1914), in which she argues strong correlations between Upaniṣadic thought and early Buddhism, and the thesis offered by I. B. Horner in her splendid *Early Buddhist Theory of Man Perfected* (London : Williams and Norgate, 1936) that "the original *dhamma*, a teaching which would appeal to every man, was transformed into a gospel in which 'stopping' (*nirodha*) was taught as a cure for ill (*dukkha*). Such was the monkish contribution to Gotama's doctrine" (p. 27ff). I also refer the reader to the thorough treatment of "causality" by David Kalupahana in his *Causality : The Central Philosophy of Buddhism* (Honolulu : The University of Hawaii Press, 1975) in which he develops a convincing argument for the original paramount importance of *paṭiccasamuppāda* in the Buddha's formulation of *dhamma*.

In this study, our focus will be on the soteriological blueprint ascribed to Gotama Buddha by early followers in a Buddhist canonical text known as the *Vinayapiṭaka.* This "basket of discipline" comprises one of the earliest extant bodies of Buddhist literature that is available to us. Like the Pāli *Nikāyas,* the *Vinaya* reflects the religious frame of reference of Gotama's early monastic followers. The text is primarily concerned with elucidating over two hundred rules of discipline that range greatly in character : from sanctions prohibiting the taking of life, stealing, engaging in sexual intercourse and lying about one's spiritual attainments to rules of seemingly minor importance which define proper clothing apparel and diet. Of almost equal importance, the text is also concerned with determining how these same disciplinary rules should be cultically celebrated within carefully specified ritual contexts. By internally cultivating a frame of reference conducive to adhering to this extended disciplinary code, the individual member of the monastic community could hope to make necessary progress "*against* the stream" of life that leads to incessant rebirth. The path of discipline leads on to the Summum Bonum of Buddhism, *nibbāna.*[1]

In addition to this expressly soteriological formula, we have already mentioned the ritual concerns of the *Vinaya.* These ritual concerns betray the fact that part of our text is removed in time and focus from other early Buddhist literature.[2] Nevertheless, the *Vinaya's* treatment of ritual addresses the crucial importance of maintaining a united and spiritually pure monastic community, a concern that no doubt antedates its canonical expression. Thus, within the *Vinaya,* we find an account of the early history of the *Saṅgha* in which the origins of the most significant monastic rites are recounted. In this carefully orchestrated account, an attempt is made to establish a spiritual basis for the charismatic identity accorded to the Buddha's monastic followers. Briefly, these ritual transactions are occasions in

1. Throughout this study, we shall use Pāli renderings of terms except where Sanskrit terms are more appropriate.

2. For instance in *Therīgāthā* (*Psalms of the Sisters*) vv. 165, 166, we find a reference to rites as being one of the five lower fetters that drag one backwards along the path. Horner believes "the taint of rites and ceremonial performances was probably included as a safeguard against brahmanical practices." See Horner, *Early Buddhist Theory*, p. 273.

which the *Saṅgha* declares its role as being the spiritual extension of and successor to the master by virtue of being the authoritative maintainer of *dhamma* and discipline.

The *Vinayapiṭaka* source, therefore, is bifocal : it defines a means by which an individual monastic adherent may achieve the soteriological goal of Buddhism and it determines the manner in which the collective monastic community may sustain its special identity. We are about to examine two blueprints that form a related whole : a soteriological strategy which pertains to the individual and a mythic charter that legitimates and sustains the community. Ultimately, it can be effectively argued that the thrust of the soteriological blueprint leads to a transcendence of concerns for the character of the community. But as we shall see, that argument is valid only from a limited perspective. The monastic community very early came to regard itself as a soteriological community in which its ultimate identity transcended its own temporal existence.

The key to understanding the ethos of the *Vinaya* source involves a serious reckoning with the message of the Buddha and the importance attached to the notion of "discipline." It will be necessary for us to reconstruct in outline form the essential elements of the Four Noble Truths before we begin our considerations of the *Vinaya* in detail. But first, a few words about the nature of discipline are in order.

The term *vinaya* usually has been loosely translated as "discipline." There really is no reason to call that translation into question as discipline, in fact, is the root concept at work in our text. However, we gain a deeper appreciation for the type of discipline characterized within the *Vinaya* if we pay attention to the literal meaning of the term. The prefix *vi* connotes "difference," "distinction," "apart," "away from," etc. When combined with the verb root $\sqrt{}$*nī* which basically means "to lead," we end up with *vi*+$\sqrt{}$*nī* meaning "to lead away from." *Vinaya*, the reified noun form of the verb *vi*+$\sqrt{}$*nī* therefore leads us to the general meaning of "that which separates," or "that which removes." Some scholars understandably have taken the term to mean that which leads away from this world.[1] This is not an

1. See for instance, Edward Conze, *Buddhism : its Essence and Development* (New York : Harper and Row, 1959), p. 54.

inappropriate rendering of the term when the monastic path is conceived of in terms of "otherworldliness." The *Saṅgha* has often been characterized as a "community not of this world." And, when one considers the Buddhist goal of ending the cycle of rebirth, this understanding of *vinaya* seems sufficient. However, we hope to demonstrate during the course of this study that translating *vinaya* to mean "that which removes" is a more accurate reflection of what is involved in the Buddhist understanding of discipline as it is reflected in our text.

Our translation of the term *vinaya* begs the question : what is being removed ? To answer that question in the simplest terms, that which is being removed are wrong states of mind, the conditions of grasping, desiring and ignorance which stem from the delusion that we have a "self" that can be satiated. The discipline of the *Vinayapiṭaka* represents a systematic assault on the *idea* of "ego-consciousness." The goal of *Vinaya* discipline is to remove such an idea, or if you will, to lead away from it. This can only be achieved by those who have experienced a type of conversion in the manner in which they perceive the world or interpret the meaning of existence. The discipline of the *Vinaya* is as important to cultivating this frame of reference as it is a product of this very mind set. The need for the circular nature of this last description will become increasingly apparent as we proceed through our analysis. In essence, the discipline of the *Vinaya* is a means to overcoming the sense of "I-ness" (*ahaṃkāra*) as the result of a conscious effort. Yet, once *ahaṃkāra* is removed, perfected external behavioral expressions need no longer be considered as the product of consciously disciplining one's mind; rather, these expressions are merely the outward reflections of one's calmed inward disposition. The best way to describe this serenity of inward disposition is *virāga* (detachment). Thus, the path of discipline advocated by the *Vinayapiṭaka* leads to a condition of detachment from the fetters of existence that generate *ahaṃkāra*. "Disciplined behavior" is none other than a characterization of the behavioral expressions of a perfected being (*arahan*). It is the hallmark of one in whom all grasping has ceased.

When we examine the teachings of the Buddha, we see that the discipline advocated by the *Vinaya* represents a very significant application of the Buddha's *Dhamma*. Indeed, throughout the

Pāli *Nikāyas,* we often find the phrase "this dhamma and this discipline" referring to the fact that the discipline advocated by the Buddha is part and parcel of his teachings. The two cannot be successfully separated if we are to gain an adequate understanding of the Buddha's soteriological message. And that is why it is so disturbing that the *Vinayapiṭaka* has been relatively neglected in academic circles. Because the *Vinaya* constitutes one of three main sections of the Pāli canon, it has always been highly revered throughout the history of Buddhist tradition by Buddhist adherents. Perhaps the *Vinaya* has been ignored by scholars because of the rather formidable format in which it is presented, or perhaps because pioneer buddhologists and historians of religions were more intrinsically interested in the more philosophically oriented *Abhidhammapiṭaka* and the more doctrinally and cosmologically oriented *Suttapiṭaka.* The importance of attaining proper knowledge or mystical insight has been rightly emphasized in studies of these collections. However, the *Vinaya's* emphasis upon proper action has been eclipsed in this process.

Early Buddhist texts present the teachings of the Buddha within the context of his Four Noble Truths. These cardinal precepts, which form the cornerstone of Buddhist doctrine, are given to us in the same manner that a doctor diagnoses a problem and prescribes a cure. However, we must keep in mind that the Four Noble Truths are not the consequence of objective abstract reflection or the product of serious rational study. Rather, they represent a description of the knowledge gained by the Buddha in his enlightenment experience. Though the teachings are explained within a discursive frame of reference, they are ultimately rooted in an existential realization. In fact within the *Suttavibhaṅga*[1] portion of *Vinaya,* the Four Noble Truths are mentioned only in passing after a thorough-going description of the Buddha's enlightenment experience. They represent a summary of the understanding that resulted from enlightenment, a fact which underscores the *Vinaya's* emphasis on experience over abstraction. Thus to begin by analyzing the Four Noble Truths without first paying heed to the experience which produced them would not only violate the spirit of our text, but would also

1. The first of two major divisions comprising the *Vinayapiṭaka.* We shall discuss the structure of the *Vinaya* at length in a following chapter.

ignore the very experience that was to become paradigmatic for Gotama's followers.

Leaving aside the prehistory of the enlightenment experience that is so elaborately developed in other sources,[1] the *Vinaya* account begins straightforwardly in its description of Gotama's mounting of the four *jhāṇic*[2] trances :

> Brahmin, I had steadily put forth energy, clear mindfulness had arisen, my body was quieted and calm, my mind was composed and one-pointed. I, brahmin, aloof from pleasures of the senses, aloof from wrong states of mind, having gained the first musing with its reflection and investigation that is born of solitude, zestful and easeful, abided therein. By the mastery of reflection and investigation, having inner faith, the mind concentrated, without reflection, without investigation, having attained the second musing that is born of contemplation, zestful and easeful, I abided therein. By the fading out of zest, I dwelt poised, mindful and attentive, and I experienced welfare as to the body, attaining the third musing which the noble ones describe in these terms : "he who is poised and mindful dwells happily," I abided therein. By the rejection of ease and by the rejection of discomfort, by annihilation of the rejoicing and sorrowing I had before, having attained to that state which is neither pleasant nor painful, that utter purity of mindfulness which is poised, which is the fourth musing, I abided therein.[3]

As our source relates, the first trance is produced by becoming detached from sense objects and detaching oneself from passions. This characterization, as we shall see, lies at the heart of discipline. Unlike the first trance, the second is non-discursive requiring total concentration or "one-pointedness." The third trance is dispassionate rather than zestful, described more as a calmful bliss. Finally, the fourth trance represents the ultimate

1. For traditional biographies of the Buddha, see the *Mahāvastu* of the Mahāsāṁghikas, the *Lalitavistara* of the Sarvāstivādins, and the *Buddhacarita* attributed to the first century A.D. poet Aśvaghoṣa. See also the Pāli *Jātakas*.

2. Sanskrit *dhyāna* (trance, meditation).

3. I. B. Horner, ed. and trans., *The Book of Discipline* (*The Vinayapiṭaka*), 5 vols. (Sacred Books of the Buddhists, Vols. 10, 11, 13, 14, and 20; London : Oxford University Press, 1938-52), 1 : 7.

stage wherein the mind is completely free from opposites, untainted, purely aware, even-minded. All the stages of meditation are characterized by concentration and accurate cognition. The insight they facilitate does not lead to theoretical knowledge, but to direct perception.[1] Or, to put it another way, the trances lead to a perceptual frame of reference wherein pure cognition can be *experienced.*

The *Vinaya* account then proceeds to describe three cognitions that the Buddha experienced during the three watches of the night. In the first instance, Gotama became aware of his own previous existences :

> Then with the mind collected, clarified, purified, void of taints, grown soft and pliable, fixed and come to utter peace, I directed the mind towards the knowledge of the memory of former becomings . . . such a one was I by name, having such and such a clan, having such and such a color, so was I nourished, such and such easeful and painful experiences were mine, so did the span of life end.[2]

During the second watch of the night, Gotama acquired paranormal vision in which he surveyed the qualitative births and rebirths of beings everywhere :

> . . . I directed the mind towards the knowledge of the arising and passing hence of beings; so that with the purified deva-vision surpassing that of men, I behold beings, I know beings as they pass away or come to be—mean, excellent, fair, foul, in a good birth, in a bad birth according to their actions. . .[3]

Finally during the third watch of the night, we are told that Gotama arrived at the knowledge for the need to destroy the "cankers" :

> . . . I directed my mind toward the knowledge of the destruction of the cankers. I knew as it really is : This is ill, this is the arising of ill, this is the stopping of ill, this is the course leading to the stopping of ill. I knew as it really is : These are the cankers, this is the arising of cankers, this is the stopping of cankers, this is the course that leads to the stoppings of cankers.

1. Richard H. Robinson, *The Buddhist Religion* (Belmont, CA : Dickenson Publishing Co., 1970), p. 18.
2. *Book of Discipline*, 1 : 7-8.
3. *Ibid.*, p. 8.

In me thus knowing, thus seeing, my mind was freed from the canker of sensual pleasure, my mind was freed from the canker of becoming, my mind was freed from the canker of false views, my mind was freed from the canker of ignorance. Freed, to me came knowledge through the freedom : I knew : Destroyed is rebirth, lived is the Brahma-life, done what is to be done, there is no beyond for this state of things.[1]

Although the *Vinaya's* account of the enlightenment experience in no way provides us with a detailed explanation of the Four Noble Truths, the central message of the Buddha's teaching is readily apparent. There is an overwhelming emphasis placed upon the need to gain control over the mind rather than allowing the mind to control the individual. The mind must be aloof, detached, calmed before the knowledges "seen" during the watches of the night can be experienced. Once this state of detachment has been attained, the ascension of the four *jhāṇic* states is understood to be one of clarification or purification. Only when one's frame of reference is *unconditioned* can one hope to perceive the true nature of existence and destroy the mental sores that ulcerate the mind.

And what is the true nature of existence that the Buddha discovered on his night of enlightenment ? He first came to the knowledge of his former becomings and then the arising and passing away of all beings according to their actions. This knowledge forms the basis for the course of action that the Buddha was subsequently to prescribe throughout his missionary career. His analysis of the nature of existence has been often referred to as the "chain of causation." The term used to designate this process is *paṭiccasamuppāda.* Since the *Suttavibhaṅga* account does not give us a detailed explication of *paṭiccasamuppāda,* we must look elsewhere within the *Vinaya* for further information as to what is involved.

The *Mahāvagga* portion of the *Vinaya,* a portion of the second of the two main divisions of literature comprising our text, begins with an alternative account of the Buddha's enlightenment experience in which *paṭiccasamuppāda* is explicated in outline :

Then the Lord during the first watch of the night paid attention to causal uprising in direct and reverse order : conditioned by

1. *Book of Discipline*, p. 8.

> ignorance are the habitual tendencies (saṅkhāra); conditioned by the habitual tendencies is consciousness (viññana), conditioned by consciousness is the psycho-physicality (nāmarūpa—name and form); conditioned by psycho-physicality are the six sense spheres; conditioned by the six sense spheres is awareness (phassa); conditioned by awareness is feeling; conditioned by feeling is craving; conditioned by craving is grasping; conditioned by grasping is becoming; conditioned by becoming is birth; conditioned by birth is old age, dying, grief, sorrow and lamentation, suffering, dejection and despair come into being. Such is the arising of this entire mass of ill. But from the utter fading away and stopping of this very ignorance comes the stopping of the habitual tendencies . . .[1]

This "chain of causation" is never ending for those who remain in ignorance. The unending cyclical nature of existence for those wallowing in ignorance has been graphically portrayed in Buddhist art as the Wheel of Life. But ignorance can be overcome through the experience of enlightenment. Through knowing the origins of suffering (*dukkha*), one can hope to break the "chain" of conditioned existence and attain to a state of freedom. We find this hope expressed time and again throughout the early Buddhist scriptures: "whatever is of the nature to uprise, all that is of the nature to stop."[2] That is to say, if the perception of the mind is conditioned in such a way as to generate actions on behalf of a "self," it is also subject to a prescribed path of discipline in which such a selfish concern can be eliminated. It is precisely this concern for the self that causes the types of actions which perpetuate incessant rebirth.

In early Buddhism, the most significant component in its anatomical view of action is volition. Actions motivated by qualitatively good intentions lead to beneficial consequences in this world and favorable consequences for one's future rebirths. Actions motivated by evil intentions have the reverse effect. However, Buddhist discipline is aimed at cultivating neither of these two types of actions with their corresponding consequences. Rather, the goal is to act in a totally detached manner without regard to the fruits of one's actions. This means that no *kammic*

1. *Book of Discipline*, 3 : 1-2.
2. *Ibid.*, p. 17.

consequences result from unintentional deeds. Herein lies the manner in which the Wheel of Life can be transcended by the disciplined follower : a disciplined detached mind, unaffected by such dispositions as passion, hatred, greed, or ignorance, will not produce a "caused," conditioned action. And once causation has been overcome, so the *saṃsāric* wheel of existence is broken, freedom is attained, "done what is to be done," etc. Adhering to the disciplinary rules of the *Vinayapiṭaka* constitutes a means by which the process of endless becoming can be arrested.

This brief portrayal of the Buddha's enlightenment experience and our few comments about the role of discipline in relation to cultivating a detached, unfettered mind give us the needed perspective to better understand what is at stake in the Four Noble Truths. Suffering in this world is caused by excessive concern for one's own self. Buddhism is often criticized for being a theory of annihilationism. This is because those making such a charge believe that the Buddha sought to annihilate the self. This is not the case; rather, the Buddha sought to eliminate the *idea* of a permanent self and set out to explain why such a concept is untenable on the one hand, and leads to suffering on the other.

Buddhism stands unique in the history of religions by denying the existence of a permanent self. To understand this argument, we must again return to the notion of *paṭiccasamuppāda*, that all beings are conditioned. Being conditioned, each entity that makes up the conditioned world is therefore impermanent : it is continually subject to changing conditions. Moreover, every "thing" in the world is made up of constituents each in turn irreducible to its "self" or essence. All "things" or "beings" are compounded. For example, when we refer to an object as a "chair," what we are really referring to is an entity composed of wood, metal, or other apparent substances that have been molded into parts (legs, seat, back and arm rests) to form the whole. Is there any one "essence" to the chair ? The Buddha answers that there is not, that what makes up the chair is the combination of apparent substances (which in turn can be broken down) molded into parts which, when fitted together, form the chair. There is no one particular substance or no one particular part that can be identified as the essence of the chair. And given time, even the form that we identify as the chair will disintegrate naturally or be taken apart with its materials used for some other purpose. So it is with the self: it is impermanent (*anicca*) and nonsubstantial (*anatta*).

Now, suffering is the consequence of striving to satisfy the desires of something that is impermanent and nonsubstantial. Here, we understand suffering in terms of the frustration that attends the individual who constantly seeks to satiate himself. As soon as one believes that he has satisfied himself or fulfilled his desires, conditions change so that a new set of desires drive him onward in his incessant quest to quench his thirst. Such a person is a slave to his passions and wallows in his ignorance. He suffers (*dukkha*), and will continue to suffer in continual rebirths as long as he volitionally generates actions that call for *kammic* retribution. To stop this cycle, the Buddha prescribed his course of training known as the Noble Eightfold Path (*ariya aṭṭhaṅgika-magga*), a calculated effort to end the cause of suffering.

The well-known Noble Eightfold Path formula[1] rests upon three elemental notions: (1) ethical conduct (*sīla*), (2) mental discipline (*samādhi*), and (3) wisdom (*paññā*). It should be emphasized that one aspect of the path is not to be taken up first or not to be practised to the exclusion of the others. It is an integrated path. In a dialogue between a *deva* and the Buddha in *Saṃyutta Nikāya* 1, 13, we find the Buddha insisting upon the integrated nature of his path :

The inner tangle and the outer tangle—
This generation is entangled in a tangle.
And so I ask of Gotama this question :
Who succeeds in disentangling this tangle ?

The Buddha's response :

When a wise man, well established in *sīla*
Developes *samādhi* and *paññā*,
Then as a bhikkhu ardent and sagacious,
He succeeds in disentangling the tangle.

A good case can be made for the fact that the Buddhist disciplinary code found in the *Vinayapiṭaka* represents an elaboration of what the early Buddhists understood as *sīla* (morality). Right

1. Right understanding (*sammā diṭṭhi*), right thought (*sammā saṅkappa*), right speech (*sammā vācā*), right action (*sammā kammanta*), right livelihood (*sammā ājīva*), right effort (*sammā vāyāma*), right mindfulness (*sammā sati*), right concentration (*sammā samādhi*).

speech (not lying, gossiping, etc.), right action (not killing, not stealing, and not engaging in sexual intercourse) and right livelihood (not taking employment that results in harm to living creatures) are said to be constitutive of *sīla*. Similarly, these concerns comprise the first four and most important rules that make up the disciplinary code as they are presented in the *Suttavibhaṅga* and the liturgical *Pāṭimokkha Sutta*.[1] Violation of these rules entails expulsion from the monastic community. Moreover, the invocation of the Mahāsāṃghika recension of the *Pāṭimokkha* declares that the collective recitation of the disciplinary code is a proclamation of the *bhikkhusaṅgha's* "pure" *sīla*.[2] Here, we would apparently have good evidence for arguing that the disciplinary code represents a detailed complement to the notion of ethical conduct. As such, the code of discipline might be considered as one of the three essential components of the Noble Eightfold Path.

But during the course of this study, we want to show that what is involved in the Buddhist notion of discipline is really much more comprehensive in scope. One cannot perfect discipline by virtue of *sīla* alone; but one must also possess knowledge (*paññā*) of the real nature of the world (*paṭiccasamuppāda*) and one must achieve clarity of mind (*samādhi*) before one can cause the fires of ego-oriented actions to wane utterly. The three aspects of the path must go hand-in-hand before the soteriological goal of *nibbāna* can be won.

Although the early texts speak of many individuals converted by the Buddha who quickly achieved the goal of *arahan*ship, other passages reveal that *nibbāna* was only gradually attained. Perhaps these varying accounts presage later Buddhist controversies that centered on the issue of whether enlightenment was to be experienced suddenly or only after considerable training. In any case, we often find passages in the *Nikāyas* referring to stages of attainment, references that reflect that at least a portion of the early Buddhist community understood the path of deliverance

1. The *Pāṭimokkha* plays an extremely important role in the development of the disciplinary code. See pp. 35-40. As a text in its own right, it is recited every two weeks at the Uposatha celebration. See pp. 39-40.

2. Charles Prebish, *Buddhist Monastic Discipline : The Sanskrit Prātimokṣa Sūtras of the Mahāsāṃghikas and the Mūlasarvāstivādins* (University Park, PA : Pennsylvania State University Press, 1975), p. 42.

as being graded. This simply indicates that some *bhikkhus* were thought to have progressed further along the path to *nibbāna* than others, or that every member of the community was not accorded the same spiritual status. It also indicates the general belief that all could not hope to achieve the goal within the span of a single lifetime. In the *Majjhima Nikāya*, we find a descending scale measuring levels of achievement for members of the community :

> Because *dhamma* has been well taught by me thus, made manifest and opened up, made known stripped of its swathings, those monks who are perfected ones, the cankers destroyed, who have lived the life, done what was to be done, laid down the burden, attained their goal, the fetter of becoming utterly destroyed, and who are freed by perfect profound knowledge—the track of these cannot be discerned.
>
> . . . those monks in whom the five fetters binding the lower (shore) are got rid of—all these are of spontaneous uprising, they are attainers of utter nibbāna, not liable to return to this world.
>
> . . . those monks in whom the three fetters are got rid of, in whom attachment, aversion and confusion are reduced, all these are once-returners who, having come back to this world once, will make an end of anguish.
>
> . . . those monks in whom the three fetters are got rid of, all these are stream-attainers who, not liable to the downfall, are assured, bound for awakening.
>
> . . . those monks who are striving for *dhamma*, striving for faith are bound for awakening.
>
> . . . all those who have enough faith in me, enough affection are bound as though for heaven.[1]

This passage found in the *Majjhima Nikāya's* "Parable of the Water" is recorded right after the Buddha has advised his followers to "put away" or remove themselves from *paṭiccasamuppāda*. It represents an early attempt to delineate between grades of achievement along the path. It should be noted that the goal of those who have achieved the highest state "cannot be discerned."

1. I. B. Horner, trs. and ed., *The Middle Length Sayings* (*Majjhima Nikāya*), 3 vols., (Pali Text Society Translation Series Nos. 29-31; London : Luzac and Company, 1954-59), 1 : 181-182.

I. B. Horner has taken this to mean that the ultimate achievement cannot be conceived of in conventional terms. It represents a "going beyond" (*pāraṅgata*).[1] But to get to that stage, one must destroy the cankers of existence, the *āsavas* and the less attending fetters. Clearly, the path is here perceived as one of purification. In a later discussion of the *Suttavibhaṅga*, we shall show in detail how the disciplinary code of the *Vinaya* is essentially a means for overcoming these obstacles that block the way to *arahan*ship.

Theoretically, it was possible for a layman to gain the highest goal if he could fulfil all of the requirements of discipline.[2] However, the life of a householder made this extremely difficult.[3] The path of the layman was predominantly characterized as a path of meritorious actions and veneration for the Buddha. Thus, as the last passage from the *Majjhima* text indicates (and it is important to note that here "monks" has been replaced by "those" so that this first grade of achievement refers to all members of the Buddhist community), those who espouse a faith and devotion to the Buddha will attain rebirth in heaven.[4] Far

1. Horner, *Early Buddhist Theory*, pp. 282-312.

2. This view is most emphatically related in *Milindapañha* IV, 6, 16, where we find Nāgasena telling Milinda : "Whether he be a layman, O brethren, or a recluse, the man who has reached Supreme Attainment shall overcome all difficulties inherent therein, shall win his way even to the excellent condition of Arahatship." Further elaboration on this point can be found in T. W. Rhys Davids, trans., *The Questions of King Milinda*, 2 vols. (Sacred Books of the East, Vols. 35-36; London : Oxford University Press, 1894), 2:56-59. But there was still considerable concern about laymen becoming "backsliders," members of the order who wished to return to conventional society. Further, if a layman did attain to *arahan*ship, it was held that he should immediately join the *bhikkhusaṅgha*. See *ibid.*, 2 : 63-75.

3. Although this was the predominant view held by the *bhikkhusaṅgha* as reflected, for instance in the *Sāmaññaphala Sutta* of the *Dīgha Nikāya*, later Buddhist tradition, especially the view put forward in the *Vimilakīrti Nirdeśa Sūtra*, did not necessarily believe that the life of the layman prevented an individual from living a life commensurate with the requirements of the path. In this *sūtra*, the central protagonist, a layman named Vimilakīrti, clearly demonstrates his superiority in terms of wisdom over the most prominent disciples of the Buddha and the foremost *bodhisattvas*.

4. For a discussion on the importance of faith as a prerequisite to attaining the goal, see Jan T. Ergardt, *Faith and Knowledge in Early Buddhism* (Leiden : E. J. Brill, 1977).

from being a consolation prize for the laity, this last statement underscores a crucial difference between lay and monastic piety. The monastic spiritual quest was based upon the destruction of the "cankers," a process involving the purification of one's mind through discipline so as to ultimately eliminate *kammic* consequences. On the other hand, the path of the laity involved a continued participation in the Wheel of Life on the basis of *kammic* consequences accruing from actions. We might say that the laity remained "merit conscious." This crucial aspect of lay piety had prodigious consequences for the nature of monastic-lay relationships.

Bhikkhus, in the development of early Buddhism and throughout the development of later tradition, represent one of the two most auspicious fields of merit for the laity. Along with the Buddha, they provide opportune occasions for improving one's spiritual status. Any action performed with good intent that takes the Buddha or his *Saṅgha* as its object will necessarily afford positive *kammic* consequences. Because the *Saṅgha* is thus specified as an auspicious field for potential merit-making, its collective status was of the utmost importance not only to the monastic community, but to its lay supporters as well. It is here that the previously mentioned public proclamations of collective purity gain added importance. And, as we shall see in our discussion of the primary monastic rituals outlined in the *Vinaya* text, collective purity is what enables the *Saṅgha* to make good its claim to be the Buddha's successor on spiritual matters.

In return for providing the laity with a "field of merit," the monks received basic material support from the laity, a feature of monastic-lay relationships that enabled the *Saṅgha* to remain not overly concerned with the mundane requirements of everyday existence. If a monk need not worry about where he could procure food, clothing and a place to sleep, he was less likely to be tempted by the allurements of the world. He was free to concentrate upon the requirements of discipline. Thus, the relationship between the monastic community and the laity was symbiotic. In effect, it fostered the belief that the *Saṅgha* was a perfected community, set apart from the orientations of this world that require grasping and material success.

These are the major issues that fit together into a paradigm for salvation and a blueprint for community as they pertain to the notion of discipline in the *Vinayapiṭaka.* Clearly, the texts bear the unmistakable stamp of monastic scholastic formulations and are beyond a doubt a remake of the Buddha's original message. They reflect a blueprint for *transcendence* of this world and a strategy for *order* within this world. There should be no mistaking the fact that they represent ideals as conceived by the early Buddhist community, the organized hopes of organized men. They contain the aspiration to ultimately transcend it all, to go beyond (*pāraṅgata*) to a state which cannot be discerned. But few men possess the drive to complete the ideal and we would be naïve to believe that the ideal represents what in fact was the real practice. The *Vinayapiṭaka*, replete with its own modifications, restructurings and enlargements, reveals that the ideal was not easily won. And even if the ideal were to be won, we find passages in the early texts that recommend that once one has succeeded in crossing over the stream, the raft that has aided one should be discarded.[1] Thus, discipline itself is not to be retained ultimately. It is only a means to an undisclosed end, *nibbāna.*

In the following pages of our study, we shall attempt to provide a detailed analysis of the issues we have raised in this brief introduction. We shall begin our probe with a discussion of the Buddhism's predecessors and contemporaries before proceeding to a description of the *Vinaya.* In following chapters, our focus will be more narrowly centered. We shall attempt to understand the fundamental ethos of Buddhist discipline on the basis of an analysis of the *Suttavibhaṅga.* In so doing, we shall determine the great importance of discipline in the *bhikkhu's* quest for *nibbāna.* By seeing how discipline was cultically celebrated according to the prescriptions of the *Mahāvagga.* we will show how adherence to discipline became central to the corporate identity of the monastic community. And finally, our conclusion will address the general buddhalogical import of discipline and the originality of discipline as a means to achieving salvation in the history of man's religions.

1. *Middle Length Sayings,* 1 : 173-74.

Chapter Two

PREDECESSORS AND CONTEMPORARIES

The path of discipline, as it is depicted in the *Vinayapiṭaka*, leads to the attainment of the soteriological goal as the consequence of a spiritual life governed by disciplined action. It is an individual quest completely dependent upon one's own ability to sustain a detached disposition. The individual is totally responsible for his own spiritual fate. This type of emphasis upon the individual's soteriological quest is indicative of the *śramaṇic* challenges to dominant *brāhmaṇical* modes of religious piety. The rise of Buddhism did not occur within an historical vacuum, but must be seen within the context of its historical predecessors and contemporaries.[1]

Brāhmaṇical religious tradition was essentially rooted in the believed efficacy of the sacrificial act. Before the appearance of Gotama and other *śramaṇa* teachers such as Mahāvīra of the Jainas and Gosala Maskarīputra of the Ājivakas, and before the beginnings of *upaniṣadic* speculations, *brāhmaṇical* religion possessed a theory of action which provided a systematic theodicy for its religious adherents. The Buddhism that we shall explore in this study represents a rejection of that theory which in turn led to a novel reconceptualization of dominant religious ideas in the history of Indian religious thought.

The ritual sacrifice of *vedic* religion was inextricably tied to the belief in personal deities who were thought to be responsible for many events of this world beyond the control of human beings. These personal gods could be placated and influenced through offerings of food and displays of reverence within the ritual sacrifice context. As the gods benefited from the sacrificial actions of their worshippers, so it was believed that the propitiators would receive a fair return for their displays of piety. The

1. Perhaps the most accessible and best summary of the *śramaṇic* challenge to *brāhmaṇical* orthodoxy can be found in P. S. Jaini, "Śramaṇas : Their Conflict with Brāhmaṇical Society," in Joseph W. Elder, ed., *Chapters in Indian Civilization*, 2 vols. (Dubuque, Iowa : Kendall/Hunt Publishers, 1970) 1:39-81.

sacrifice was an appeal to the gods to be gracious in granting boons and in maintaining the world.

At a crucial point in the history of *vedic* religion, a subtle, yet fundamental change occurred in the understanding of *vedic* sacrificial actions. We find the emerging belief that if the sacrifice were performed in precise manner according to carefully specified prescriptions, a predictable consequence would necessarily follow. This understanding signals the introduction of a mechanistic theory of cause and effect. Types of actions could be counted on as generating desired effects. The favor of the gods was no longer needed ! Sacrificial action alone produced the desired result. This understanding appears as the prevailing notion in later *vedic* religion reflected by the ritual texts known as the *Brāhmaṇas*. The implementation of this theory of cause and effect is none other than the application of magical knowledge. That is to say, with proper knowledge of the dynamics of the universe, the sacrificer may hope to seize control of the forces of nature. The actor/protagonist of the ritual sacrifice becomes the manipulator of the environment. Thus, man's role in the cosmos becomes centered upon his duly performed sacrificial action. The primary consequence of his sacrificial action was the maintenance of the world. In this conserving schema, man functions as the decisive factor in the ongoing process of the universe. In other words, man has taken over the role formerly ascribed to the gods. J. A. B. van Buitenen has described this important development in the following way :

> Although the *Yajamāna*, the Sacrificer, is a specific individual, when he is involved in his rite, he is the *epitome* of all men. As the ritualistic speculations develop, we see that side by side with the two principal terms, the cosmos and the sacrifice, a third term begins to be introduced, that of the sacrificer himself. It is not only the sacrifice that is in the closest communion with the cosmos, that generates the power which keeps the cosmos going ("if one does not perform the *agnihotra* at dawn, the sun will not come up"), now it is also man *himself*. Man constitutes himself a microcosm that mirrors the macrocosm.[1]

1. J. A. B. van Buitenen, "*Vedic* and *Upaniṣadic* Bases of Indian Civilization," in Elder, *Chapters in Indian Civilization*, p. 17.

He goes on to say that

> The parallelism between macrocosm and microcosm, between universe and man is so complete that not only can the world at large be viewed in the image of man, but also the creation of the world can be viewed as the creation of man.[1]

In the *Śatapatha Brāhmaṇa*, we are told that this elevated importance of man as the creator and maintainer of the universe is dependent upon man's knowledge of how to perform the specific actions (*karma*) of the sacrifice. This knowledge, previously utilized solely by the gods and believed to account for their immortality, is now within man's province. Thus, it presents man with one possibility of achieving his own immortality. As the cosmos can be eternally maintained, so man, a mirror of the cosmos, can maintain his own eternal being.

In the following passage from the *Śatapatha Brāhmaṇa*, Māra (Death) complains that this special knowledge acquired by man has robbed him of his role. The gods' response to Māra constitutes a formal statement about the crucial importance of possessing sacrificial knowledge :

> Death spoke to the gods : surely thus all men will become immortal. Now what will be my share ? They said : henceforth no other shall be immortal with his body, but only when thou shalt have taken the body as thy share. Thus having parted with the body he shall be immortal who is to be immortal through knowledge or karma. Now in that they said this : through knowledge or karma, it is the fire-altar that is the knowledge, and this fire-altar that is karma. So that they who know this, or they who do this karma, having died are born again, thus being born again they are born again to immortality. They who do not know or they who do not know this karma, on dying again, they become the food of Death again and again.[2]

Within this passage, we find an early statement regarding the doctrines of action and retribution as well as transmigration and rebirth. *Karma* is here referred to as the dynamic of sacrificial action. Knowledge of this karma is what divides those who

1. van Buitenen, "*Vedic* and *Upanişadic* Bases," p. 18.
2. *Śatapatha Brāhmaṇa* X. 3. 4-10; E. J. Thomas, *The History of Buddhist Thought* (London : Kegan Paul, Trench, Trübner and Co., 1933), p. 108.

"know" from those who do not "know" and as such, those who attain immortality and those who do not.

This important distinction made in the *Śatapatha Brāhmaṇa* indicates what separated the *brāhmaṇical* class from the rest of society. That is to say, by being born into a special class, an individual inherited the special knowledge of his fathers : a clerical elitism was enforced by the institution of inheritance. In one sense, a biological model of community is at work here. Knowledge of *karma,* that special quality needed to attain immortality, was the exclusive province of a segment of the community that was passed on from generation to generation. Within this context, *karma* had yet to be linked to moral and ethical concepts. However, the principle of cause and effect had been established and the notion of retributions which span over more than one lifetime had been predicated.

Reincarnation was heavily contemplated as *brāhmaṇical* orthodoxy moved into the period of *upaniṣadic* speculation. The doctrine of rebirth or reincarnation was extended in two ways. Cosmologically, it was believed that a human being could be reborn as an animal, as a god, or into some other form of life as the consequence of his actions. Good actions would result in favorable rebirths, bad actions in a less desired state. Quality of one's actions became the new theodicy explaining various grades of life. Here, morality and ethics did assume great importance in connection with *karmic* retribution. Philosophically, the notion of *karma* was abstracted from its specific ritual context and generalized to apply to all actions of the individual. Although the importance of sacrificial action was not totally eclipsed in this reformulation, it was no longer held to be the only arena in which consequences of the soteriological or cosmological type could be affected. Rather, all man's actions were considered to have efficacy in determining the quality of one's future existence. One effect of this reformulation was that access to the Summum Bonum of religion was opened up. The priestly *brāhmaṇical* class no longer could, in effect, monopolize the business of immortality. And thus, we find the emergence of another type of holy man who was not dependent upon knowledge of sacrificial action for his salvation. This holy man is the wandering *bhikṣu,* one who has renounced the world in search of eternal salvation.

We must remember that the idea of microcosm-macrocosm was still exercising full force in the minds of India's holy men during the period of the *Upaniṣads.* In fact, it reached the zenith of its expression while at the same time generated a new theory of how salvation could be achieved : knowledge of the true nature of the "self." The man without this knowledge "is composed of desire, in proportion to desire is his will, in proportion to his will he performs acts, and according to his aots does it happen to him."[1] And so a man is reborn according to the nature of his deeds. But generally, the goal of the aspirant in *upaniṣadic* sources is not heavenly reward for good deeds. Rather, the goal is the realization of one's own self (*ātman*) with the universal "self" of existence (*Brahman*). Emancipation from rebirth is achieved when one attains the knowledge of the unity of the self with the absolute. He who knows "I am Brahman" in effect becomes the universe. He who knows the supreme *Brahman*, the ontological essence of the universe, becomes *Brahman.*[2] In this schema, knowledge constitutes deliverance. Man ceases to be affected by desires of any kind and so his deeds no longer have any effect upon him.[3] "Like the reed stalk in the fire, his works consume themselves away."[4] This knowledge, that one's own essential being is identical with the essence of the cosmos, is that which leads to the eternal experience of unity within an existence that appears to be diverse in form. All apparent multiplicity is but illusion. And, it is this saving knowledge which redeems the individual from the constant stream of births. The expression "Thou are that" enunciates the fundamental belief that all existence is an indivisible unity.[5] And it is this very "self" which participates in and constitutes this unity.

Several motifs that we have discussed in connection with the *Upaniṣads* also find expression within early Buddhism. For instance, Buddhism fully accepted the theory of cause and effect as well as the notion that the quality of one's actions bear qualitatively upon one's future spiritual or cosmological status.

1. A. B. Keith, *Religion and Philosophy of the Veda and Upaniṣads*, 2 vols. (Cambridge : Harvard University Press, 1925), 2 : 574.
2. *Muṇḍaka Upaniṣad* III. 2. 9.
3. *Bṛhadāraṇyaka Upaniṣad* IV. 4. 22.
4. *Chāndogya Upaniṣad* V. 24. 3.
5. Ibid., VI. 8. 7.

We also find in early Buddhism a stress upon the need to transcend the efficacy of one's deeds if one is to achieve the final goal. But as we shall see, the means by which *karmic* retribution is overcome within the Buddhist context is quite different. In addition, the earliest followers of the Buddha were of the *bhikṣu*[1] type mentioned in the *Upaniṣads*.

As compelling as some of the comparisons appear to be, we cannot lose sight of the fact that Buddhism arose as one of several small sects that challenged the very basis of *brāhmaṇical* orthodoxy. Whereas the *Upaniṣads* constitute a brilliant reformation of *brāhmaṇical* orthodoxy, Buddhism and other *śramaṇa* sects amount to a vigorous rejection of *brāhmaṇ*ism.

In the period from the eighth through the fifth centuries B.C., the Aryanized *brāhmaṇical* traditions, which had been firmly established in northwestern and north India, were gradually making their way eastward into the Gangetic River Valley, the area in which Buddhism was to originate.[2]

Such *brāhmaṇical* ideas as *dharma*, *karma*, and *ātman* were given new evaluations and significance upon their importation. Types of religious practices including *yoga* and asceticism were incorporated in this new context by semi-*brāhmaṇical* or non-*brāhmaṇical* systems. With regard to types of holy men, groups of wandering mendicants, mentioned previously in connection with *Upaniṣadic* sources of the *vedic-brāhmaṇical* tradition, became ever more numerous and influential.[3]

These religious developments were accompanied by a rapid disintegration of traditional tribal patterns and political authority. The introduction of iron, the emergence of intense agricultural cultivation, and urban centers serving expanding trade and commerce, all contributed to a reorganization and re-evaluation of traditional understandings of religion and society. Charles Drekmeier has suggested that this breakdown of long established

1. Pāli : *bhikkhu*.

2. For an excellent scenario of this development, see D. D. Kosambi, *An Introduction to the Study of Indian History* (Bombay : Popular Book Depot, 1956).

3. For a still commanding treatment of the ethos of these mendicants, see Sukumar Dutt, *Early Buddhist Monachism* (London: Kegan Paul, Trench, Trübner and Co., 1924).

patterns represented a "tribal trauma."[1] Smaller kingdoms were absorbed into larger political units and with the establishment of these greater geographical areas of political hegemony, travel became more easily facilitated. In short, this period of Indian history in northeast India was one of great change and instability. More than one scholar has suggested that a sense of despair must have accompanied these sweeping changes as the impermanence of life became heavily contemplated.[2] Significantly, it was within this milieu that the radically new *śramaṇic* religious orientations made their appearance proclaiming new hopes for overcoming suffering.

Although each *śramaṇa* sect proclaimed a specific doctrine, they all shared a common rejection of traditional *brāhmaṇical* modes of authority. The *vedic* sources of inspiration were rejected. The caste system was disregarded and membership in *śramaṇa* groups was open to anyone regardless of caste position. Unlike the emphasis placed upon knowledge in *upaniṣadic* speculations, *śramaṇa* teachers advised that one must *act* in prescribed manners by means of disciplined self-effort in order to gain salvation. In other words, emphasis was placed upon what a man must *do* or *not do* rather than upon what he must know.

Three of these groups, the Buddhist, the Jainas and the Ājīvakas represent the most successful *śramaṇic* challenges to the dominant *brāhmaṇic* religious ethos. Both the Ājīvakas and the Jainas are mentioned in the early Buddhist texts. An understanding of both of these positions will help to clarify the Buddhist argument within the context of the *śramaṇic* challenge.

The theory of Maskarīputra Gośala, founder of the Ājīvakas and a former disciple of Mahāvīra of the Jainas, is recorded briefly in the *Dīgha Nikāya* in the *Sāmañña-phala Suttanta* :

When one day I had asked Makkhali of the cow-pen, he said : "There is, O king, no cause, either ultimate or remote, for the

1. Charles Drekmeier, *Kingship and Community in Early India* (Stanford, CA : Stanford University Press, 1962), p. 63.

2. Frank Reynolds, "The Two Wheels of Dhamma : A Study of Early Buddhism," in Bardwell Smith, ed., *The Two Wheels of Dhamma* : *Essays on the Theravada Tradition in India and Ceylon* (Chambersburg, PA : The American Academy of Religion, 1972; American Academy of Religion Studies in Religion, Number 3) : 9-10; Thomas Hopkins, *The Hindu Religious Tradition* (Belmont, CA : Dickenson Publishing Co., Inc., 1970) : 52-3.

> depravity of beings; they become depraved without reason and without cause. There is no cause, either proximate or remote, for the rectitude of beings; they become pure without reason and without cause. The attainment of any given condition, of any character, does not depend either on one's acts, or the acts of another, or on human effort. There is no such thing as power or energy, or human strength or human vigor. All animals, all creatures (with one, two, or more sense), all beings (produced from eggs or in a womb), all souls (in plants) are without force and power and energy of their own. They are bent this way or that by their fate, by the necessary conditions of the class to which they belong, by their individual nature : and it is according to their position in one or another of the six classes that they experience ease or pain.[1]

This theory of "fatalism" or natural determinism was considered from the Buddhist point of view as constituting one of the worst forms of sophism. The Buddhists charged that if everything that occurs in existence is the consequence of fate, species and natural laws, no room is left for human determination or moral responsibility for one's actions. "Fatalism" also dismisses the theory of *karmic* retribution. As such, the Ājīvaka position, which advocated extreme forms of asceticism as a means of "blocking out suffering," constitutes a theory of external causation of suffering. Suffering is not the consequence of one's own spiritual condition. The Buddhists traditionally regarded the Ājīvaka position as a form of nihilism. This criticism is stated in the early Buddhist texts in the following way :

> One acts, another experiences the result—this, Kassapa, which to one smitten by feeling occurs as "suffering caused by another," amounts to the Annihilationist [uccheda] theory.[2]

In this context, *uccheda* refers to the annihilation of the belief

1. *Dialogues of the Buddha* (*Dīgha Nikāya*), T. W. and C. A. F. Rhys Davids, trans. and eds., 3 vols. (London : Luzac and Co., 1899-1921; Sacred Books of the Buddhist, Vols. 2-4) 1:71; for a fine elucidation of this passage, see Kalupahana, *Causality*, pp. 32-40.

2. *The Book of Kindred Sayings* (*Saṃyutta Nikāya*), C. A. F. Rhys Davids and F. L. Woodward, trans. and eds., 5 vols. (London : Oxford University Press, 1917-30; Pāli Text Society Translation Series, Nos. 7, 10, 13, 14 and 16) : 2 : 16.

that actions have consequences for the actor. Although this may appear to be a similar doctrine to the one advocated in the *Vinaya*, it does not, in fact, take into account the importance of the individual's own efforts. It is, rather, an argument that denies the role played by discipline. Everything that is caused is the consequence of forces that lay outside of the individual. This position annihilates the importance of disciplined actions. It is quite a different doctrine from the one posited in the *Vinaya* where that which is annihilated are the "manifold evil and wrongful states," passion (*rāga*), hatred (*dosa*) and ignorance (*moha*).[1]

The Buddhists regularly depicted their own position as being a "middle way." Usually, this is taken to mean the middle position of moderation between hedonism on the one hand and rigorous asceticism on the other. But, it may be more accurate to understand the Buddhist argument as the middle position between eternalism (as advocated in the *Upaniṣads*) and annihilationism (as advocated by the Ājīvakas).[2] The depiction of existence as impermanent, conditioned, and generated according to the *paṭicca-samuppāda* formula prevented the Buddhists from accepting the metaphysical idea of a permanent, eternal self. The doctrine of *anatta* runs contrary to the *upaniṣadic* belief in ultimate *self*-realization. On the other hand, the Ājīvaka position denies the efficacy of causal determination, control of which lies at the heart of Buddhist discipline.

It might be argued that the Jaina theory of action is closest to the understanding of the Buddhists. Indeed, a passage from the *Vinaya* indicates that the Buddhists were more tolerant of the Jaina and Jaṭila positions. If a *bhikkhu* had left the *Saṅgha* to join another *śramaṇa* group and returned desiring to be re-admitted, he was usually required to spend four months of probation.[3] However, if the *bhikkhu* had defected to the Jainas or Jaṭilas, the four months of probation was waved.

> And for what reason? These, O Bhikkhus, hold that actions receive their reward, they affirm what ought to be done.[4]

1. *Book of Discipline* 1 : 3-5 and 4 : 321.
2. Kalupahana, *Causality*, p. 142.
3. This probationary status is the *mānatta* discipline. See *Book of Discipline* 4 : 85-88.
4. Ibid., p. 89.

If the Buddhist theory of causation can be understood as a middle way between the two extremes of annihilationism and eternalism, then the Jaina argument might be seen as an attempt to combine the notions of self-causation and external causation. It was Mahāvīra's contention that the nature of existence is neither completely caused by the self, nor is it totally the result of destiny or fatalism. Rather, he says :

> Those who proclaim these views [eternalism and annihilationism] are fools who fancy themselves learned; they have no knowledge and do not understand that things are partly determined and partly undetermined.[1]

By this, the Jainas meant to say that internal causes such as human exertion as well as external factors such as time, God, nature and *karma* may interact relative to the total context. By *karma*, the Jainas were referring to the past efficacy of actions that bear fruition in the present. And although the Jainas admitted the factor of indeterminism, they managed to insist that past actions do result in determinism. This may appear to be contradictory, but indeterminism was understood as one of those factors that condition *karmic* consequences relative to a specific context in which they gain fruition.

That is to say, one's past actions may function as a cause for consequent developments, but these developments are also tempered by the relativity of the occasion textured by time, space, etc. Thus both self-causation and external causation produce the present. Or to put it another way, once a man commits an action, the determinism resulting from that action becomes external to him, beyond his control. Thus, he both causes his future by past actions and then is determined by them. The Buddhists depicted the Jaina theory thus :

> Whatever this individual experiences, whether pleasant or painful or neither pleasant nor painful, all is due to what was previously done. Thus by burning up, by making an end of ancient deeds, by the non-doing of new deeds, there is no overflowing into the future. From there being no overflowing into the future comes the destruction of deeds; from the destruction of deeds comes the destruction of anguish; from the destruction of anguish comes the destruction of feeling;

1. Cited in Kalupahana, *Causality*, p. 46.

> from the destruction of feeling all anguish will become worn away. Jainas speak thus . . .[1]

Again, we have encountered a theory that appears to be very similar to the Buddhist understanding. But there are crucial differences between the two positions. In the first place, *karma* is understood in Buddhist texts not as an external factor of causation. Rather, it is understood as volition.[2] Secondly, the Buddhists did not advocate non-action to eliminate further accumulation of *karma*; they advocated detached, disciplined actions. Thirdly, there is the "devastating" criticism aimed at the Jainas in a continuation of the passage cited above in the *Majjhima Nikāya* :

> If, monks, pleasure and pain which creatures undergo are due to what was previously done, certainly, monks, the Jainas were formerly doers of deeds that were badly done in that they now experience such severe, sharp feelings.[3]

What follows from this passage is the accusation that if the Jainas are so intent upon eradicating evil, they must have committed manifold evil deeds in the past. The pain that Jainas now experience in their austerities might be seen as due reward for past actions. Finally, the Jainas understood *karma* to be a substance that adheres to one's soul, discoloring its natural purity. This substance is the product or result of actions. In effect, the Jainas argued that action produces substance. Unlike the Jainas who sought to eradicate this *karmic* substance through asceticism and non-action, the Buddhists understood *karma* to be a mental cause that results in outward expressions of behavior. As such, the Jaina understanding of *karma* may be taken as a materialistic perspective as opposed to the processive understanding inherent in the Buddhist notion of *paṭiccasamuppāda*.

Our survey of pre-Buddhist religious thought reveals that the Indian religious mind was continually and creatively engaged in organizing soteriological aspirations. Buddhism accepted as many ideas from its predecessors and contemporaries as it rejected.

1. *Middle Length Sayings* 3 : 3.
2. *The Book of Gradual Sayings* (*Aṅguttara Nikāya*), F. L. Woodward and E. M. Hare, trans. and eds., 5 vols. (London : Oxford University Press, 1930-36; Pāli Text Society Translation Series Nos. 22, 24-27) : 291-295.
3. *Middle Length Sayings* 3 : 10.

While rejecting the *vedic* orthodoxy of *brāhmaṇism*, it accepted the belief emanating out of the ritual sacrifice context that actions produce consequences, and that man, rather than the divine, plays the most important role in the forging of personal destinies. It assumed that actions of all types, and not just actions performed within the arena of sacrifice, require retribution—a debt owed to *upaniṣadic* speculations. And, in accordance with Yājñavalkya, Buddhism agreed that *karmic* retribution must be transcended if the ultimate goal is to be achieved. However, as part of indigenous reactions to *brāhmaṇic* culture in a period of social and political instability, Buddhism joined with other *śramaṇa* groups in challenging the authority of the *Vedas*. Consequently, it disregarded *brāhmaṇical* theories of the "self" and society. Along with other contemporary *śramaṇic* orientations, Buddhism stressed a course of action, or an ethic of discipline rather than placing ultimate confidence in the attainment of knowledge as the chief means of achieving the soteriological goal. Unlike the "eternalism" of self-causation promoted by the Ājīvakas, Buddhism assumed a middle course by positing its doctrines of *anatta*, *anicca*, and *paṭiccasamuppāda*. But instead of attempting to forge a synthesis of "eternalism" and "annihilationism," an endeavor that led to the Jaina path of penitential austerities and a doctrine of non-action, the Buddhists argued for an ethic of detachment and discipline in the performance of actions, the training of the mind and the acquisition of wisdom.

It is precisely this ethic of discipline that played such a decisive role in the early history of the Buddhist community. Thus far, our discussion has been focused upon a comparative history of Indian religious ideas germane to the central concepts of importance in the early Buddhist texts. But it is essential that we now turn to a discussion of the evolution of the *Vinaya* source and the significance accorded to it in the early epochs of Buddhist history.

Chapter Three

THE *VINAYAPIṬAKA* : HISTORY AND STRUCTURE

I. B. Horner, who has translated the *Vinaya* in its entirety so that it is now available to us in a six volume critical edition, tells us that "the two essential points to grasp in connection with original Buddhism are that, in the first place, the 'texts' do not date from Gotama's time, but are about two centuries later; and that in the second place, they are very largely the fruits of monkish labor."[1] Horner and others have marshalled evidence to suggest that between the time of the Buddha's death and the period in which the canon was formed, the teachings of the Buddha were modified from an ethic aimed at a continual self-perfection of "becoming" to a syndrome in which "Monastic Buddhism craved a wholesale making to cease."[2] According to Sukumar Duṭt, monastic modifications were not limited to the understanding of the goal to be achieved, but also involved a reconsideration of the significance of the master. While trying to delineate between the "folk memory" of the historical Gotama and the later evolving notion of the "Buddha-concept," he asserts that "in the transference of materials from popular tradition to monkish legends, there was a transmutation as thorough as there could be. The legends broke with the tradition, not only in linguistic medium, but also in form and spirit."[3]

It is difficult to share the anxiety expressed by Horner and Dutt. There is no reason to bemoan the fact that Buddhism underwent transformations in its early history. Rather, these changes only represent religious man's continual effort to re-shape, remold, or enlarge upon the visions of his predecessors. It does noṭ necessarily follow that these endeavors must be considered antithetical to the ethos of earlier tradition or constitute a "counterfeit Buddhism" camouflaging the untainted

1. Horner, *Early Buddhist Theory*, p. 32.
2. Ibid., p. 283.
3. Dutt, *The Buddha and Five-After Centuries* (London : Luval and Co., 1957), p. 10.

original truth. The fact of the matter is that the texts now at our disposal are inspired by the manner in which the Buddhist community understood the nature of the Buddha's message and its applicability to their own individual and corporate spiritual quests. Such an understanding was conditioned by space and time dating to a period when the religious community that claimed Gotama as its founder was settling down to the business of becoming an organized community.

The *Vinaya* is the product of one highly regarded attempt to define membership in that community, a serious reckoning with the central concern of "what it means to be Buddhist." The reformulation of ideas into a new structure of understanding is but a natural reaction of emerging communities in a time when the founder has perished and the generation of his immediate disciples is no longer present to clarify ambiguities that inevitably arise. Needs for clarification or systematizing appear whenever new communities become geographically and socially diffused. If a community is successfully expanding, the original brotherhood that formed around the master is soon transcended in time and space. In this process, Joachim Wach writes that "charisma and seniority [of the founder and his disciples respectively] have now become insufficient for authority. A reorganization sets in, discipline is established, and the brotherhood is ended, to be succeeded by a new type of organization, the ecclesiastical body."[1] It is at this point of development that we find the significant role played by the *Vinayapiṭaka* in the early history of Buddhism. The text consists of a systematic endeavor to specify the means by which *nibbāna* might be won and a definition of the community that supports such a goal. If we agree that our text reflects religious aspirations of the soteriological kind, then it should not be overly difficult for us to consider the expressions of monastic Buddhism as authentic aspirations no more or no less "religious" than the original message of the Buddha, whatever it may have been.

That the earliest Buddhists were a wandering lot is amply testified to in the early Buddhist sources. The emphasis upon wandering surfaces in many passages. In the *Dhammapada*, for instance, we read :

1. Joachim Wach, *Sociology of Religion* (Chicago : The University of Chicago Press, 1944), p. 141.

Who is a Brahmin ? He is a Brahmin
who stays away from the well-housed and the houseless,
who does not live in houses, and has few wants.[1]

In our own text, the *Vinayapiṭaka*, the master exhorts his disciples to wander individually for the welfare of all beings :

Walk, monks, on tour for the blessing of the manyfolk, for the happiness of the manyfolk out of compassion for the world, for the welfare, the blessing, the happiness of devas and men. Let not two of you go by one way.[2]

The only apparent break in the *bhikkhu* life-style came during the period of *vassa*, the rainy monsoon season. But, as Charles Prebish has observed, "this custom was certainly not distinct to the Buddhists, but rather was observed by many sects within the *parivrājaka* community, two examples being the Jainas and the Brāhmaṇical Sannyāsins."[3] The reasons for the temporary halt in wandering are well-known. The onslaught of continuously heavy rain made travel very difficult and "by this time too the Jaina notion of *ahiṃsā* or noninjury compounded the problem, for many small forms of life would fall prey, even inadvertently, to man's crude efforts at rainy season travel."[4]

It is highly probably that the practice of suspending wandering for three months gradually led to the suspension of wandering in general. Several factors were probably responsible for this transition from an eremitic to a cenobital life-style. Nomadic people return each year to known safety and sustenance. And, it is not difficult to imagine that once a *bhikkhu* had found a convenient place to spend the rains, he would return to the same place year after year. References in the *Vinaya* indicate that very early on, monks joined together to build temporary buildings of a rather crude nature in order to secure shelter during *vassa*. Such cooperation marks the beginnings of the monastic experience. By living together for three months at a time, no doubt there were many opportunities to share spiritual insights, cultivate formal relationships with the laity, and establish daily routines that in time became reified. The building of an *āvāsa*, the term

1. *The Dhammapada*, P. Lal, trans. (New York : Farrar, Strauss and Giroux, 1967), p. 174.
2. *Book of Discipline* 4 : 28.
3. Prebish, *Buddhist Monastic Discipline*, p. 4.
4. Ibid.

denoting these crude shelters, is specifically outlined in the *Vinaya*[1] indicating that communal regulations soon followed the establishment of these communities. Another type of monastic buildings, *ārāmas*, seems to have been of a more permanent nature. These structures were built by the laity and donated to *bhikkhus* for their own uses. Gradually, *ārāmas* begin to be called *vihārās* (connoting a greater sense of permanence) and other buildings forming campuses of monastic complexes are also mentioned in *Vinaya* literature.[2]

In addition to references to these types of buildings, the *Vinaya* also hints at an increasing structure of organization within the confines of these buildings. Prebish shrewdly notes that the *Vinaya* mentions the assignment of beds within these buildings three times : the first time at the beginning of the monsoon season, the second time for one month after the rains had begun, and a third time at the conclusion of the rainy season.

> The Cullavagga . . . describes this third assignment as antaramuttaka or intervening, with reference to "the next rainy season." Since assignments for the next rainy season could easily be accommodated at that time, this third assignment is superfluous. The third assignment simply exists because monks did not wander randomly, settling down with their friends and companions with the onset of the rains, wherever

1. The third chapter of the Mahâvagga (*Book of Discipline* 4 : 183-207) is dedicated to "its [*āvāsas*] construction, maintenance, regulations for living within it, and also manners and points of etiquette to be observed." Sukumar Dutt, *Buddhist Monks and Monasteries of India* (London : George Allen and Unwin, Ltd., 1962), pp. 58-59. Emphasis upon the details for constructing *āvāsas* is demonstrated in the particular care required for the establishment of *sīmās* (boundaries) so that no two *āvāsas* overlap territorially or infringe upon the private property of householders. S. J. Tambiah has suggested that the establishment of these boundaries "separates out and encloses a sacred space of 'limited' extent vis-à-vis the vast secular space of the village and town." *Buddhism and the Spirit Cults of North-East Thailand* (Cambridge : Cambridge University Press, 1970), p. 71. Cf. Jacque Maquet, "Expressive Space and Theravâda Values : A Meditation Monastery in Sri Lanka," *Ethos* 3 (Spring, 1975) : 1-21.

2. See *Book of Discipline* 4 : 187-88 and 5 : 96-140. Dutt has described in general terms the nature and function of these auxiliary buildings in his *Early Buddhist Monachism*, pp. 184-92.

they might be, but rather returned to the dwelling place of the previous year(s).[1]

Reference to permanent communities in the *Vinaya* indicate that much time could not have elapsed before the eremitic life-style had been completely abandoned in favor of established and settled *saṅghas* which then became the norm. Prebish believes that this shift in life-style took place within one hundred years after the death of Gotama.[2] Sukumar Dutt is of the opinion that settled communities were established within fifty years of the founder's decease.[3] Thus, it would seem credible that the disciplinary code embodied within the *Vinaya* source probably began to make its appearance in one form or another as settled communities began to ponder rules for the regulation of life within. A discussion of the structure of the *Vinaya* will lead us closer to assigning an approximate time during which the disciplinary code was formulated.

The *Vinayapiṭaka* of the Pāli school of Buddhism has been completely preserved. Modern scholarship has recovered fragments or portions of five other *Vinayas* representing the texts of the Sarvâstivâdins, Dharmaguptakas, Mahīśāsakas, Mahāsāṃghikas, and Mūlasarvâstivâdins. All *Vinayas* are somewhat similar in structure. Typically, these extant versions are divided into two distinct sections : rendered in the Pāli text as the *Suttavibhaṅga* (division of *suttas*) and the *Khandhaka* (chapters).[4]

The materials of the *Suttavibhaṅga* are organized around each of the disciplinary precepts that make up the collective disciplinary code. These precepts comprise the monastic regulations which govern proper social behavior, attire, food, medicine and etiquette. Before each rule is explicitly stated in the text, a brief story has been included to provide the context in which the rule was initially laid down. These stories make up the most

1. Prebish, *Buddhist Monastic Discipline*, pp. 8-9.
2. Ibid., p. 23.
3. S. Dutt, *The Buddha*, p. 10.
4. Hirakawa argues that the *Suttavibhaṅga* of the Pāli *Vinaya* represents the oldest version of the first part of *Vinayapiṭaka* that has survived. He bases his assertion on the fact that the Pāli recension contains the least amount of *apadāna* material when compared to other texts. Hirakawa considers *apadānas* to be a genre of literature from a later period. See Hirakawa, *A Study of the Vinaya* (Tokyo : Sankibo-Busshorin, 1960), pp. 12-15.

entertaining literature in the *Suttavibhaṅga.* In every case, an errant *bhikkhu* behaves in some mischievous manner that requires the establishment of a rule to prohibit such occurrences from taking place in the future. It is within these stories that we shall be able to gain a clear understanding of the ethos of our source.[1] Following the declaration of the rule which comes at the end of each story, a detailed commentary is appended which carefully defines the exact wording of the rule's declaration so as to precisely clarify the intent and applicability of the rule in question. After the commentary, we usually find a series of stories which illustrate how the factors of intent, conspiracy, actual completion of the act, and types of participants (men, women, ghosts, animals, etc.) all serve to require modification of the rule or strict application. These last materials reflect the monastic understanding of jurisprudence. All of the rules with their "embroidering" materials have been organized into seven sections according to the severity of the penalty for transgressing each of the rules. Thus, the most heinous offences, together with their stories and commentaries, are listed first in the text's sequence. An eighth section constitutes a brief account of ways to settle disputes. Since we shall be referring to these rules frequently in later discussions, it would be helpful to characterize them in cursory fashion.

The first section of rules presented in the *Suttavibhaṅga* includes the four *pārājikas*, violation of which involves permanent expulsion from the monastic community. These are the most serious offences that a *bhikkhu* could commit : (1) sexual intercourse of any kind, (2) "taking what is not given," (3) taking of human life or conspiring to do so, and (4) falsely claiming to have achieved a superior spiritual status. The second section is comprised of thirteen *saṅghādisesa* rules that refer to offences that require the offender to spend a period of penance before he can be reinstated by a formal act of the *bhikkhu* order. Five rules deal with minor sexual offences, two with properly constructing *bhikkhu* dwellings, two with bringing false accusations against

1. Rhys Davids and Oldenberg believe that these introductory stories may have provided later biographers with the materials they needed to formulate their biographies of the Buddha. *Vinaya Texts*, T. W. Rhys Davids and Hermann Oldenberg, trans. and eds., 3 vols. (London : Oxford University Press, 1881; Sacred Books of the East, Vols. 13, 17 and 20) 1 : xviii-xxi.

fellow *bhikkhus*, two with causing dissension within the order, and two with insubordination. The third section contains two "undetermined" (*aniyata*) cases in which an offender might be charged with the breaking of one or another of the rules in the disciplinary code, depending on the nature of the offence. Specifically, they refer to types of transgressions that can occur if a *bhikkhu* were to sit in a secluded or non-secluded place with a woman. The thirty *nissaggiya pācittiya* rules make up the fourth section and require "expiation and forfeiture" if transgressed. Although *bhikkhus* were not permitted to have any personal possessions, four requisites (a set of robes, a bowl, a bed, and medicine) were considered indispensable. These particular rules prevent the *bhikkhu* from obtaining outright possession of these requisites or any other article and serve as reminders that everything ultimately belongs to the collective order. The ninety-two *pācittiya* rules are included in the fifth section. They represent a miscellany of concerns intended to promote harmony among *bhikkhus* and to help the individual avoid leading a life of luxury that might distract him from progressing along the path. The sixth set of rules, the *pāṭidesaniyas*, are four precepts governing etiquette while making almsrounds. If one of them is broken, the offender need only confess his wrong-doing. And finally, the seventh section of rules referred to as the *sekhiyas* are the most minor in nature; although, as we shall see, they sparked a grand controversy in early Buddhist history. For the most part, they deal with the daily routine of the *bhikkhu*, his behavior while making almsrounds, his behavior while preaching *Dhamma* to the laity, while eating, etc.

This same list of rules with the exclusion of the appended stories and commentaries, is also contained in the *Pāṭimokkha*[1]

1. The Pāli term "*pāṭimokkha*" (Sanskrit "*prātimokṣa*") has caused considerable confusion in the attempt to render a standard definition. The Monier-Williams dictionary of Sanskrit gives the meaning of *prāti+mokṣa* (from *mokṣ*, the desiderative form of √muc) as "deliverance, liberation." Rhys Davids and Oldenberg agree to render the word to mean "to free oneself, to get rid of," *Vinaya Texts*, 1 : xxvii-xxviii. E. J. Thomas also favors a meaning derived from √*muc* but translates it as "that which binds, obligatory," *The History of Buddhist Thought*, 2nd ed. (London : Routledge and Kegan Paul, Ltd., 1963), p. 15, note 1. Winternitz associates the word with "redemption," Maurice Winternitz, *A History of Indian Literature*, 2 vols., (Calcutta :

Sutta, a liturgical formula recited every two weeks at the Uposatha ceremony. Hermann Oldenberg was of the opinion that the *Pāṭimokkha* "is the earliest specimen of Buddhist *Vinaya* literature that we possess."[1] The very close relationship between the *Pāṭimokkha* and the *Suttavibhaṅga* becomes apparent when we notice that all of the rules, word for word, appear in both texts. This fact led Oldenberg to conclude that the "whole Vibhaṅga is nothing more than an extended reading of the *Pāṭimokkha*."[2] But an important question is then begged : is the *Pāṭimokkha* an abstracted summary of the disciplinary code or is the *Pāṭimokkha* the more ancient of the two texts having generated the *Suttavibhaṅga* as an explanatory excurses ? Oldenberg argues that the second of the two possibilities is the most likely because the *Pāṭimokkha*, without an appended commentary and illustrations, reads as an uninterrupted whole, that the commentary and illustrations of the *Suttavibhaṅga* point to a later origin because they represent a further extension in the applicability of the rules, and that the *Mahāvagga* and *Cullavagga* portions of the *Khandhaka* division presuppose the existence of the *Pāṭimokkha* and account for the origins of its recital.[3] If we agree with Oldenberg, and we can find no other evidence that would contradict his speculation, then we can assume that the *Pāṭimokkha* not only is the root of the *Suttavibhaṅga*, but it is also older than the second part of the *Vinaya*, the *Khandhaka*.

While the *Suttavibhaṅga* stands in closest relation to the ancient *Pāṭimokkha*, there was a new and wider circle of *Vinaya* discipline added to the rules we have just described, the *Khandhaka*, put together probably about the same time that the *Suttavibhaṅga* was framed. In that effort, redactors endeavored to go beyond the scope of the *Pāṭimokkha* rules in order to provide the monastic community with a coherent picture of ideal *saṅgha* life. They

University of Calcutta, 1927, 1932), 2 : 22, note 2. W. Pachow offers "each, every" for *prāti* and "liberation, deliverance" for *mokṣa*, *A Comparative Study of the Prātimokṣa*, Sino-Indian Studies IV and V (1951 and 1955) : 20. Finally Sukumar Dutt offers his unique definition by rendering *prātimokṣa* as "bond." He arrives at this meaning by rendering *prāti* as "against" and *mokṣa* as "scattering", *Early Buddhist Monachism*, pp. 88-90.

1. Hermann Oldenberg, ed. with introduction, The *Vinaya Piṭakam*, 5 vols. (London : Williams and Norgate, 1874), 1 : xv-xvi.
2. Ibid., p. xvi.
3. Ibid., pp. xvii-xx.

provided a history of the founding of the order by the Buddha, a detailed account of the *Upasampadā* ordination procedure, specified prescriptions for properly conducting the annual rituals held at the end of the *vassa* season,[1] an account of the origins and procedures for the *Pāṭimokkha* ritual, and a description of the first two Great Buddhist Councils. The titles given to the two sections which make up the *Khandhaka* are *Mahāvagga* and *Cullavagga*. As in the *Suttavibhaṅga* literature, the structure of the text is arranged so that every declaratory statement is enshrined in a brief story. Oldenberg regarded these stories as "pure invention."[2] According to Oldenberg, both portions of the *Vinaya*, the *Suttavibhaṅga* and the *Khandhaka*, were likely composed at roughly the same time and the only significant difference between each part of the text is that the *Suttavibhaṅga* elaborations were added to a pre-existent disciplinary code (the *Pāṭimokkha*), while the *Khandhaka* was composed completely at one time.[3]

It is not necessary that we completely agree with Oldenberg's assessments, especially with regard to his suggestion that the *Khandhaka* was transcribed in one setting. But it is important that we address ourselves to the origins of the disciplinary rules as they appear in the *Pāṭimokkha Sutta* before we make any assessment about when the *Vinaya* reached its own root form.

Although it is impossible to determine an exact date for the origins of the *Pāṭimokkha Sutta* and thus the first existence of a fully codified disciplinary code, we can point to some developments noted by other scholars that suggest an approximate period when this process was taking place.

In Sukumar Dutt's seminal study of *Early Buddhist Monachism*, the then young Indian scholar proposed that

> The Buddhist Saṅgha existed originally as a sect of the Parivrājaka community of the sixth century B.C. and it rested on the basis of a common Dhamma and had at first no special Vinaya of its own. It is impossible to say at what point in time, but certainly very early in its history, the sect of the Buddha. . .devised an external bond of union : it was called *Pāṭimokkha*.[4]

1. The *Pavāraṇā* and *Kaṭhina* rituals.
2. Oldenberg, The *Vinaya Piṭakam*, p. xxiii.
3. Ibid., pp. xxii-xxiii.
4. Dutt, *Early Buddhist Monachism*, pp. 86-87.

Dutt contends that *Pāṭimokkha* originally did not refer to a disciplinary code *per se*, but rather to a syndrome referred to in other early Buddhist texts, specifically the *Dhammapada* (verses 184-186) and the *Mahāpadāna Sutta* (3, 28) of the *Dīgha Nikāya*. His translation of the passage is presented here :

> The Buddhas call patience the highest penance,
> Long-suffering the highest Nirvāṇa;
> For he is not a mendicant who strikes others,
> He is not a Samana who insults others.
> This is the rule of the Buddhas :
> Abstinence from all sins, the institution of virtue, the inducement of a good heart.[2]

As Dutt has noted, this passage suggests that the *Pāṭimokkha*, as it was understood by the mythical Buddha Vipassi in the *Mahāpadāna Sutta*, was regarded as a confession of faith.[3] The *Mahāvagga* also seems to understand the *Pāṭimokkha* in the same light. In *Mahāvagga* II, 1-5 (Book of Discipline 4:130-137), we find that King Bimbisāra would like to see the Buddha and his *bhikkhus* preach their *dhamma* on the day of *Uposatha* like the rest of the *paribbājjakas*. The Buddha obliged, preached a discourse and declared that his *bhikkhus* should meet fortnightly on the *Uposatha* occasion. But when the *bhikkhus* gathered again, they only sat in silence while other groups promulgated their teachings. The Buddha's *bhikkhus* were chastised by the laity for being "like the dumb, or like hogs." Thereupon Gotama decreed that on every *Uposatha* occasion henceforth, his *bhikkhus* would recite the *Pāṭimokkha*. Though the text regards the *Pāṭimokkha* as a liturgical formula to be recited, it also reflects what might have been the earlier equation of *Pāṭimokkha* with *Dhamma* as Dutt has suggested. In short, the history of the *Pāṭimokkha* begins with a confession of faith and then proceeds to become an elaboration of what constitutes the practical application of that faith in terms of discipline. Only when discipline became reified did it begin to be cultically celebrated as liturgy.

Dutt seems to think that the *Pāṭimokkha*, functioning as a bond or confession of faith in a particular *dhamma*, was transformed into a disciplinary code shortly following the Buddha's

1. Ibid., p. 87.
2. Ibid., pp. 87-88.

death. He bases his contention upon his interpretation of what transpired at the alleged First Council at Rājagaha according to the *Cullavagga* :

> The canonical account of this "council," as I have already suggested, cannot be relied upon. It is based on a vague tradition of what happened in the long, long past. But we may read it between the lines. In the reported proceedings, the term, Pāṭimokkha, is nowhere mentioned, but all the heads of misdemeanour on the part of a bhikkhu are listed except the Sekhiyas and the procedural rules of Adhikaraṇa-samatha. The reason for the studied omission of the word Pāṭimokkha is not far to seek if we assume that at the time when the proceedings were put into shape, the Bhikkhus understood by Pāṭimokkha something quite different from a code of Vinaya rules... The code, whatever its original contents, became after the First Council the bond of association of the Buddhist bhikkhus, and was called Pāṭimokkha (Bond). Thus the old name for a confession of faith came to be foisted on something new, a code of Prohibitions for a Bhikkhu.[1]

But some scholars hold that this code of prohibitions was not necessarily the invention of the early Buddhists. Pachow has noted the similar nature of the fundamental moral laws of the early Jaina community as compared with the four *pārājikas* (which form the first section of both the *Pāṭimokkha* and *Suttavibhaṅga*).[2] On this point, Pachow notes that

> Gautama Buddha, of course, was a reformer in some respects but as the conventional conception of morality had been so well-established before his time, he simply had to accept their principles and cast new rules in order to suit the requirements of his disciples. . .[3]

1. Cited in Prebish, "The Prātimokṣa Puzzle : Fact versus Fantasy," *Journal of the American Oriental Society* 94 (1974) : 170.

2. Hermann Jacobi and Hermann Oldenberg are probably responsible for Pachow bringing this point to light. See Jacobi, ed. and tr., *Jaina Sutras* (Sacred Books of the East, Vol. 25) (reprinted, Delhi : Motilal Banarsidass, 1968), pp. xii-xiv and Oldenberg, *Buddha* : *His Life, His Doctrine, His Order*, trans. by William Hoey (London : Williams and Norgate, 1882), p. 332.

3. Pachow, *A Comparative Study of the Pratimokṣa* (Santiniketan : Sino-Indian Cultural Society, 1955), p. 81.

Having read these accounts, Prebish asserts that after the Buddha's death and probably during any kind of "first council," the *bhikkhus* gathered together to make these precepts into a code. Prebish refers to other early texts including the *Majjhima Nikāya* which contain the phrase "constrained by the restraints of the *Pāṭimokkha.*" These references reflect the existence of a very early code known as *Pāṭimokkha.*[1] Finally, when we compare the number and content of the disciplinary rules as they have survived in various recensions of the *Pāṭimokkha Sutta*, we notice a striking absence of dissimilarity. Table 1 below illustrates how very few alterations in the disciplinary code were allowed by various schools of Buddhism despite the fact that schism came early in the history of the tradition.

Table 1

THE DISCIPLINARY CODE ACCORDING TO EXTANT VERSIONS OF THE *PĀṬIMOKKHA SUTTA*

School	*Rules Classified by the 8 Categories of Offences*								
	I	II	III	IV	V	VI	VII	VIII	Total
Sarvāstivāda	4	13	2	30	90	4	113	7	263
Mūlasarvāstivāda	4	13	2	30	90	4	98	7	248
Dharmaguptaka	4	13	2	30	90	4	100	7	250
Mahiśāsaka	4	13	2	30	91	4	100	7	251
Pāli	4	13	2	30	92	4	75	7	227
Mahāsāṃghika	4	13	2	30	92	4	66	7	218

Our table reflects a remarkable similarity in terms of the structure and content of these various versions of the *Pāṭimokkha*, and as such, allows us to make the observation that almost all of the disciplinary code had been universally accepted in Buddhism before the beginnings of Buddhist sectarianism.

The extreme importance of the disciplinary code in the early epochs of Indian Buddhism is evident not only when we determine the apparent unwillingness to alter the content and number of rules, but also when we consider the fact that the first schism in

1. Prebish, "The Prātimokṣa Puzzle," p. 170.

Buddhism is reported to have been the result of a disagreement over specific disciplinary rules. A glance at Table 1 reveals that the greatest discrepancy between extant recensions of the *Pāṭimokkha* lies in the number of *sekhiya* (Sanskrit : *śaikṣa*) rules constitutive of the seventh category of rules of training. Prebish and Nattier have convincingly argued that this discrepancy in *sekhiya* rules lies at the heart of reasons for schism between the Sthavira faction of monks and the Mahāsāṃghikas at the Second Great Buddhist Council held around one hundred years after the decease of the Buddha.[1]

Another study by Erich Frauwallner which seeks to establish the nature of the earliest *Vinaya* literature places the framing in the first *Vinaya* source around the time of the Second Great Buddhist Council. By means of an exhaustive comparison of surviving fragments of *Vinaya* literature, Frauwallner made an extended effort to reconstruct the original content of a root *Vinaya* source. He finds three constants within the various texts : disciplinary rules accompanied by explanations and definitions (the *Suttavibhaṅga* materials), biographical materials referring to the birth and career of Gotama, and accounts of the first two Buddhist councils. After a series of comparative comments with regard to these materials found in the various recensions, he offers this lengthy conclusion about the framing of the *Khandhaka* and hence the original *Vinayapiṭaka* :

> At the time of the compilation of the old Skandhaka work about 100 years after the Buddha's Nirvāṇa the Buddhist tradition had already reached an advanced stage of development. A collection of sacred scriptures, including the Dharma and the Vinaya, was already in existence. The Vinaya included the Prātimokṣa, narratives of the type of the Vibhaṅga and much material on the monastic rules, which the Buddha was said to have communicated to his disciples. The collection of the Sūtras, which existed on its side, was handed down by a regular machinery of

1. See Prebish and Janice J. Nattier, "Mahāsāṃghika Origins : The Beginnings of Buddhist Sectarianism," *History of Religions* 16 (February, 1977) : 237-272. Essentially, these two scholars believe that the schism at the second council resulted from unwarranted expansion of the disciplinary code on the part of the Sthaviras. This is a novel reconceptualization of what happened at this council as Theravāda tradition has it that the *Mahāsāṃghikas* were at fault for being lax in discipline.

transmission, and we can ascertain a number of texts which belonged to it already in that period.

On this basis the author of the Skandhaka created his work. In doing so he was inspired by the model of the Vedic collections, which he wished to confront with something of equal standing. He gathered the whole material on the Buddhist monastic rules into a great well-planned unity. Above all, he gave it a solid cohesion, by fitting it into the frame of a biography of the Buddha. He began with the life of the Buddha till his illumination and the gaining of the first disciples. Then he told step by step how the Buddha was induced to give to the monks the precepts which form the monastic rules. The bulkiness of the material limited him in many long passages to dry enumerations. In the intervals he tried again and again to subdivide and to enliven the whole through lengthy tales and inserted legends. At the end he narrated the death of the Buddha and the compilation of the sacred texts on a first council. A list of teachers was intended to witness the validity of the tradition and credibility of the text. In his work he utilized everything out of the ancient tradition that appeared to him serviceable. He employed stories from the commentaries to the Prātimokṣa and included some Sūtra texts, which he modified according to his needs. Above everything there stands his own accomplishment and his great, almost artistic power of formation. And thus he created a work which looks imposing, if we imagine it in its original shape, and which hardly found a match in his times : the first great literary work of Buddhism.[1]

Scholarly reaction to Frauwallner's hypothesis has been mixed. The proposal that the redactor of the original *Vinaya Khandhaka* actually framed the text within a biography of the Buddha had been based upon the fact that extensive biographical material (including material from the *Mahāparinibbāna* Sutta) is strategically positioned in all but one of the preserved recensions. Etienne Lamotte has argued that although all but one of the recensions contains extensive biographical materials, the antiquity of those materials cannot be firmly established, especially in the

1. Erich Frauwallner, *The Earliest Vinaya and the Beginnings of Buddhist Literature* (Rome : Institute Italiano per il Medio ed Estremo Oriente, 1956; Serie Orientale No. 8), pp. 153-54.

case of the *Vinaya* of Mūlasarvāstivādins.[1] A number of Indian scholars, particularly G. De, reacted adversely to Frauwallner's contention that the traditions of the First Great Buddhist Council were "invented."[2] However, Frauwallner's proposition that the

1. Etienne Lamotte, *Histoire du bouddhisme indien* (Louvain : Publications Universitaires, 1958), pp. 195-197.

2. For Frauwallner's explicit statement with regard to the First Great Buddhist Council, see Frauwallner, *Earliest Vinaya*, p. 65. De's acceptance of the historicity of the First Council is found in his *Democracy in the Early Buddhist Saṃgha* (Calcutta: University of Calcutta, 1955), p. 4. But André Bareau seems to agree with Frauwallner when he says that "sometimes one even has the impression that the recitation of the council at Rājagaha has been inspired by the history of the second council and that its author wished to justify the authenticity of the canon...in order to support the condemnation of the monks of Vaiśālī, sanction of which was founded precisely on the canonical texts...in order to prevent all future dissidence in giving the community a body of scriptures which held authority." André Bareau, *Les premiers conciles bouddhiques* (Paris : Presses Universitaires, 1955), p. 28. The translation of Bareau's passage belongs to Prebish who also provides a very handy summary of scholarly comments on the Buddhist councils in his "A Review of Scholarship on the Buddhist Councils," *Journal of Asian Studies* 33 (February, 1974): 239-254. Other scholars have approached the problem of the First Great Buddhist Council by examining the content of its account in the Pāli *Vinaya.* As far back as 1908, R. O. Franke was following the 30 year old lead of Oldenberg that the account of the First Great Buddhist Council could not be taken seriously as historical. He claimed that it was "irrational" to believe that the accounts of both the 1st and 2nd councils could have been written with any degree of accuracy in such a brief time (immediately after the convening of each council). See his "The Buddhist Councils at Rājagaha and Vesali as Alleged in Cullavagga XI, XII," *Journal of the Pāli Text Society* 8 (1908) : 68. In the same year, Louis de la Vallée Poussin suggested that the account of the First council could not be really considered "historical," but that the episodes within the account pertaining to Ananda, Purāṇa, and Channa seem to be of high antiquity. He conceded that it was entirely possible that some type of council or meeting was convened to settle matters left unattended by the Buddha. See his "The Buddhist Councils," *Indian Antiquary* 37 (1908) : 17-18. Finally, thirty years later, Jean Przyluski offered a unique and new interpretation of the First council in his *Le concile de Rājagṛha* (Paris : Paul Geunther, 1926-28). He proposed that the real meaning of the council did not rest upon the question of its historicity, but instead in its cultic symbolism. By that, Przyluski was referring to the establishment of two very important rituals designed to maintain the social and cosmic order of the universe. The story of Ananda's dismissal is connected with the first of these rituals which takes place at the end of the rainy season. By forgiving Ananda his faults at the end of convocation

redactor of the *Vinaya* had used the device of tracing back precepts through the authority of eminent disciples of the Buddha (so as to confirm authority to the text) seems to be well-founded. As far back as 1915, Sylvain Levi collected materials from the various *Vinaya* texts in an attempt to show the *vedic* influence upon early Buddhist texts. Levi demonstrated the nature of that influence by comparing the structure of the early Buddhist texts to the *Upaniṣads*. In the case of both Buddhist and *upaniṣadic* texts, Levi discovered that each type always provided "contextual occasions" for each specific precept and that by placing the precept into the mouth of a venerated figure, great authority could be confirmed.[1] Finally, with reference to Frauwallner's assertion that the *Skandhaka*, and thus the completed version of the original *Vinaya*, was composed around 100 years after the Buddha's death, we again become embroiled in a rather complex discussion.

Frauwallner believes that the second Great Buddhist Council, unlike the First Great Buddhist Council, was indeed a bona fide historical event that resulted in a schism between the Sthaviras and the Mahāsāṃghikas because of a dispute over the disciplinary code. Thus, he finds in this historical event a perfect occasion for the framing of an authoritative text to settle future disagreements. He is therefore led to conclude that :

> This enables us to reach an even closer approximation in the datation of the old Skandhaka text. It must have been composed shortly before or after the second council. And since the tradition places this event in the year 100 or 110 after the Nirvāṇa, the composition must go back to about 100 years after the Nirvāṇa, that is in the first half of the 4th century B.C.[2]

and by celebrating the community's purity at the same time, the community is cleansed (for Przyluski, the rainy season represents a "purifying process"). The second story which relates the death of Gavaṃpati signifies the death of the God of aridity and the beginning of the fertile season when the *Dhamma* can be effectively preached. Thus, Przyluski's understanding of the first council is based upon his speculation that the stories of Ananda and Gavaṃpati represent mythological explanations of the two important Buddhist rites which take place at the end of the rainy season (signifying communal purity) and the beginning of the rainy season (signifying fertility).

1. Sylvain Levi, "Sur la recitation des primitive textes bouddhiques," *Journal Asiatique* (1915) : pp. 401-447.
2. Frauwallner, *Earliest Vinaya*, p. 67.

One can agree with Frauwallner that the framing of the *Vinaya-piṭaka* took place during this approximate period. That part of Frauwallner's conclusion has not been seriously disputed by reputable scholars. However, the manner in which he arrives at his conclusion can now be considered a rather gross simplification. The date of the Second Great Buddhist Council is, in fact, a matter of serious dispute. Moreover, as we shall soon see, we cannot simply refer to the Second Great Buddhist Council as a singular event; but rather, there is evidence to suggest that more than one important inter-*bhikkhu* dispute occurred during this period. As early as the late 19th century, H. Kern suspected that the origins of the Mahāsāṃghika community were not necessarily connected to that event in total.[1] As it has turned out, several other scholars have noted that Mahāyāna sources contain references to "Mahadeva's five theses" (which represents a doctrinal dispute over the spiritual status of an *arhat* or perfected being) in connection with the schism that allegedly occurred at the Second Great Buddhist Council. Theravāda accounts of the council mention only a dispute over "10 points of controversy" resulting from laxity in discipline. In that Theravāda account, those monks accused of being lax in discipline are labelled as the predecessors of the Mahāsāṃghikas. It is here that Prebish and Nattier clarify matters by a detailed examination of the sources at hand. Their conclusion confirms the fact that schism in the early history of Buddhism first resulted from disagreements over what rules should be included in the *Pāṭimokkha* code and *Vinaya* rules.[2]

The role of discipline in the early history of Buddhism is therefore of the most extreme importance. Buddhist discipline accompanied the rise of settled monastic communities in a period of time no more than one hundred years following the death of Gotama. So highly regarded was this newly evolved system of discipline that few alterations were tolerated, and those few minor rules under discussion sparked such a heated exchange that an irreversible schism resulted. These two observations point to the elevated position of discipline in early Buddhist

1. H. Kern, *Manual of Indian Buddhism* (Varanasi : Indological Book House, 1968), pp. 103-109.
2. Prebish and Nattier, "Mahāsāṃghika Origins," pp. 238-239.

monasticism. In short, it was this ethic of discipline that represented the transformation of the original message of the Buddha.

With these historical considerations in mind, we can proceed to a study of the content of this ethic as it has been preserved in the most complete recension of the *Vinaya* available to us : the Pāli *Vinayapiṭaka.* Our first task is to examine the content of the *Suttavibhaṅga* in detail in order that we can reconstruct the soteriological hope that it implicitly expresses. We can then begin a study of principal rituals outlined in the *Khandhaka* that express the cultic dimension of salvation by discipline. In so doing, we can understand the religious impulses at work in this material produced so painstakingly as "the fruits of monkish labor."

CHAPTER FOUR

MORALITY AND LEGALITY IN THE *SUTTAVIBHAṄGA*

With the major issues of our study now introduced and historical contexts provided in which to view the early Buddhist monastic movement in general and *Vinaya* literature specifically, we can now proceed to a more thorough-going analysis of our text. In the next two chapters, we shall attempt to discern the conceptual basis of discipline and determine the manner in which it relates to the soteriological path of early monastic Buddhism.

As we took stock of the types of rules encountered in the *Suttavibhaṅga*, we noted how these rules vary greatly in content and scope. The *Suttavibhaṅga* and its companion, the *Pāṭimokkha Sutta*, contain rules ranging from the highly ethical concerns of the *pārājikas* to the seemingly minor rules of comportment and etiquette found in the *sekhiyas*. With such a vast scope, there can be no easy solution to the problem of what holds the disciplinary code together. As a matter of fact, one of the brightest and most creative scholars in Buddhist studies has recently remarked that "Buddhist law is casuistic : it enunciates no broad principles from which individual rules are derived, but rather seeks to make an exhaustive listing of individual cases, each traditionally decided by the Buddha himself, to cover every single contingency of conduct."[1] The author of this statement is wise enough to know that any attempt to discern the fundamental basis of Buddhist discipline may lead to negative results. And indeed, this very chapter ends on a negative note. Before we present our own attempt to locate the importance of discipline for Buddhist soteriology and the collective image of the *bhikkhu-saṃgha,* two alternative ways of viewing the basis of discipline will be examined. In the first instance, we shall examine the hypothesis that Buddhist law can be understood correctly as a type of positive law : laws commanded by an unimpeachable source that are valid precisely because their source cannot be

1. Stephen Beyer, *The Buddhist Experience : Sources and Interpretations* lmont, CA : Dickenson Publishing Co., 1974), p. 69.

called into question. In the second instance, we shall review the adequacy of considering the disciplinary rules as being rooted in moral concerns; or to put it another way, of viewing the disciplinary rules as being elaborations of *sīla*. There is considerable merit in both of these approaches. However, both approaches fail to seriously reckon with the understanding of discipline intrinsic to the *Vinaya* source. In looking ahead to the next chapter, we shall see that it is necessary to understand the nature of action as it is depicted within the *Suttavibhaṅga* before any claims as to the centrality of Buddhist discipline can be made.

The significance of legality for our study lies in our answer to the basic questions : If Buddhist law is traditionally understood to be the result of the Buddha's casuistry, on what basis did he render judgments as to rights and wrongs of *bhikkhu* behavior ? And, on what basis did the *bhikkhu* community accept these judgments ?

Taking up the latter question first, there can be no discounting the fact that Buddhist adherents throughout the history of the tradition have venerated the *Vinaya* because most of it is considered to be *Buddhavācanā* (sayings of the Buddha). Yet, anyone familiar with Buddhist literature knows that the same claim is made for almost every other piece of Buddhist canonical literature. The principle operating with regard to *Buddhavācanā* is this : if a teaching can be ascribed to the Buddha, it is therefore authoritative. This particular concern for legitimacy surfaces throughout the histories of both Hīnayāna and Mahāyāna traditions. We have already mentioned Sylvain Levi's assessment in this regard. To this day, Theravādins hold that their canon, of which our text is a significant part, constitutes the "way of the ancients" —an unaltered preservation of the original teachings of the historical Gotama. As we remember, their claim in connection with the Second Great Buddhist Council was that the Mahāsāṃghikas had deviated from the accepted norm of discipline previously established by the Buddha. In Mahāyāna tradition, concern for an authentic basis of the teachings contained in their *sūtras* resulted in the introduction of the idea of *upāya* (the "skilful means" employed by the Buddha to preach levels of truth corresponding to the abilities of his listeners to understand; thus, the *dharma* made known to Hinayānists was a lower truth in comparison to the truths revealed in later Mahāyāna sources).

The Mahāyānists also divided the teaching career of the Buddha into stages that reflect the various degrees of insight expressed in the variety of texts that have been preserved.

Legitimating a teaching by appealing to supreme authority is by no means a facet of religion limited to Buddhist tradition. In the Christian and Islamic traditions, the legitimacy of the Bible and the Koran is reinforced by belief that these texts are the veritable "word of God." Yet, the Buddhist scriptures are not considered to be revelations from on high. If we seek more precise parallels in Christianity and Islam, we are better off to mention the tradition of *hadith* in orthodox Islam whereby authoritative teachings are traced back through a line of eminent teachers to the Prophet Muhammad or to one of his immediate disciples. In Roman Christianity, the idea of teachings passed down through apostolic succession represents a similar kind of appeal to accepted authority. No doubt, the motivation for generations of *bhikkhu Vinayadhāras* and *bhāṇakas*, whose charge it was to orally recite and transmit the teachings of the *Vinaya*, is to be found in their belief that their text was considered *Buddhavācanā* and therefore authoritative beyond question.[1] From this perspective, Buddhist law is legitimate because of the status accorded to its source.

To students of Western law, the idea that a law is legitimate because it is derived from an unquestioned authority sounds a familiar note. The intellectual grandfathers of legal positivism argued from this very position. In 1832, John Austin published his *The Province of Jurisprudence Determined*, a classic work that has been considered as providing leading opposition to proponents of natural law. As opposed to natural law, Austin argued that positive law is composed of commands requiring specified conduct that are issued from a sovereign to members of an "independent political society" over which the sovereign governs. Commands issued by the sovereign are obeyed and legitimate precisely because their source cannot be called into question.[2]

Historically, we must remember that Austin's arguments are

1. E. W. Adhikaram, *Early History of Buddhism in Ceylon* (Colombo : D. S. Puswella, 1946), pp. 24-32.

2. See John Austin, "A Positivist Conception of Law," In Joel Feinberg and Hyman Gross, eds., *Philosophy of Law* (Belmont, CA : Dickenson Publishing Company, 1975), pp. 16-28.

concerned with reinforcing the rule of monarchy. And, rationalizations of this sort really do not begin with John Austin, but can be found historically wherever imperial power employed a network of bureaucrats and scribes to administer and reinforce their rule. Indeed, a good deal of mythology has been generated so as to reinforce the unquestioned authority of imperial offices, or to provide what Max Weber has called "charisma of the office."[1]

We have raised this issue of authority because it provides us with one possible answer to our queries about the basis of Buddhist law and the disciplinary code. If the *Vinaya* rules of discipline are considered valid because they have been issued from an unquestioned authority (i.e., the Buddha), then a case can be made that Buddhist law is positive law. If this is true, then the Buddha's rules of discipline can be understood in the same vein as laws declared by a ruling sovereign : valid because they have been commanded.

To test the viability of this perspective, we need to consider the issue of kingship and authority as it is depicted in early Buddhist literature. Our findings will be compelling, but somewhat problematic.

In the *Mahāvagga* portion of the *Vinaya*, there is a story recounted in which King Bimbisāra requests that the Buddha's *bhikkhus* postpone their observance of the *vassa* rain retreat for one month. The Buddha then addresses his followers with the prescription : "I prescribe, O bhikkhus, that you obey Kings."[2] Now, this prescription can be easily misinterpreted. As a matter of fact, kings did not exercise absolute authority over communities like the Buddhist *Saṅgha*. Rather, as Sukumar Dutt has pointed out,

> The concept of society in the political philosophy of ancient India was that of an aggregate composed of units of diverse kinds—learned bodies, village communities, religious corporations, etc. Each was regarded as subject to its own conventional system of law, called *Samaya* (Conventional Law) in ancient Indian Jurisprudence. With regard to these units of society, it was the king's constitutional duty to see that none

1. Max Weber, *Sociology of Religion*, ed. Talcott Parsons, trans. Ephraim Fischoff (Boston : Beacon Press, 1963), pp. 2-3, *passim*.
2. *Book of Discipline* 4 : 184-185.

of them suffered from internal or external disruption and that the established system of conventional law of each was not transgressed. Among these societal units, the Buddhist Saṅgha became one, an "association group" functioning under a system of law of its own.[1]

Thus, the king's role is understood to be that of an enforcer who intervenes only for the purpose of preserving order. In the *Aggañña Suttanta* of the *Dīgha Nikāya*, a text that we will return to in our discussion of morality, we find that the first king, Mahā Sammata, was elected to enforce *Dhamma* among the various levels of society.[2] But law as such does not derive from him; the king's role is only to uphold the law. Thus, groups like the Buddhist *Saṅgha* governing themselves as "independent polities" were free from intervention unless they caused a disruption of order in society-at-large by failing to keep their own houses in order. For the Buddhist *Saṅgha*, *Vinaya* discipline provided a means by which the community could be self-regulated. As the king was charged with maintaining righteousness and justice in the secular world, so did the authoritative prescriptions of the Buddha regulate the sacred world of Buddhist monasticism.

The parallelism between king and Buddha is evident in a wide variety of early Buddhist texts where the authority of the Buddha is expressed through the medium of royal images. Keeping in mind the issue of sovereign law in relation to the *Saṅgha* as an "independent polity," we need to briefly address this connection between royalty and the Buddha.

In the *Mahāpadāna Suttanta* of the *Dīgha Nikāya*,[3] the career of Vipassi, the first of all the Buddhas, is represented as archetypal for all Buddhas who are to follow, including Gotama. The description relates how a Buddha descends from Tusita heaven to be born in miraculous fashion. Each Buddha is endowed with thirty-two distinctive bodily markings characteristic of a *Mahāpurisa*, a "great man" who is destined to become either a Buddha or a universal king (*cakkavatti*). The account then narrates the events of the Buddha's enlightenment and the preaching of his first sermon. In preaching the first sermon,

1. Dutt, *Buddhist Monks and Monasteries*, pp. 80-82.
2. *Dialogues of the Buddha* 3 : 88-89.
3. Ibid., 2 : 4-41.

the Buddha sets into motion the Wheel of Dhamma, an act which is the "prerogative par excellence of a universal monarch."[1] We also find material in the *Mahāparinibbāna Suttanta* of the *Dīgha Nikāya* where the Buddha is explicitly related to royal imagery. When Ananda inquires of the Buddha as to how the Buddha will be buried, the Buddha replies by telling Ananda that *bhikkhus* ought not to be concerned with this question since the Buddha will leave his *Dhamma* and *Vinaya* as a memoriam; but also, that the laity will provide funeral rites for him in the style of those accorded to a universal monarch.[2]

Clearly there is some justification for viewing the Buddha's authority in terms of royal sovereignty. The Buddha rules over the religious life according to the norms of his *Dhamma* and *Vinaya.*[3] And, the role of a sovereign seems aptly illustrated in *Suttavibhaṅga* literature. In case history after case history, we are presented with stories which illustrate how some wayward *bhikkhu* commits an action that does not conform to the norm. The matter is brought before the Buddha who chastises the *bhikkhu* in question and establishes a precept consistent with furthering the religious life. We may understand the Buddha's judgments as intervening actions designed to correct the situation at hand : to maintain order within the *Saṅgha* while at the same time promoting the private religious quests of individuals. Yet, if we are to understand the Buddha's authoritative judgments in this manner, we must also realize that the Buddha *per se* is not the source of law, but rathe only a figure who makes judgments and thereby maintains order according to an appeal to the norm he has *recognized* as valid. We must understand that the real protagonist of *Vinaya* literature is not the Buddha, but the disciplined life he advocates. The Buddha's judgments represent interpretative applications of this norm upon which discipline is built. Therefore, the *Vinaya* rules are legitimate not

1. Reynolds, "The Two Wheels of Dhamma," p. 14.
2. *Dialogues of the Buddha* 2 : 78-191.
3. The best extensive explications of the relationship of royal sovereignty and Buddhahood are Frank Reynolds' 1970 Ph.D. dissertation for the University of Chicago, *Buddhism and Sacral Kingship*; S. J. Tambiah, *World Conqueror, World Renouncer* (Cambridge : Cambridge University Press, 1976); E. Sarkisyanz, *Buddhist Backgrounds of the Burmese Revolution* (The Hague : Martinus Nijhoff, 1965); and B. G. Gokhale, "Early Buddhist Kingship," *Journal of Asian Studies* 26 (November, 1966): 15-22.

because the Buddha sits on the seat of judgment, but because they are applicable to realizing the *Summum Bonum* of the religion.

Now, if we turn to the literature of the *Suttavibhaṅga* with an eye towards determining a pattern in which these judgments are made, we can begin to catch a glimpse of the principles at work in applying discipline. We will see that these judgments were made on the basis of determining whether or not a *bhikkhu*'s actions were properly or improperly motivated. Or in other words, judgments were based upon a consideration of a *bhikkhu's* inward disposition in relation to the "spirit" of the norm. We can see this pre-eminent concern at work in the following representative case history drawn from the *Saṅghādisesa* section of the *Suttavibhaṅga.*

> At one time the enlightened one, the lord, was staying at Sâvatthī in the Jeta Grove in Anâthapindika's park. Now at that time the venerable Seyyasaka led the Brahma-life, dissatisfied. Because of this he was thin, wretched, his color bad, yellowish, the veins showing all over his body. The venerable Udâyin saw the venerable Seyyasaka thin, wretched, his color bad, yellowish, his veins showing all over his body. Seeing him thus, he said to the venerable Seyyasaka : "Reverend Seyyasaka, why are you thin, wretched... the veins showing all over your body ? Perhaps it is that you, reverend Seyyasaka, lead the Brahma-life, dissatisfied ?"
>
> "It is so, your reverence," he said.
>
> "Now then, you reverend Seyyasaka, eat as much as you like, sleep as much as you like, bathe as much as you like : eating as much as you like, sleeping as much as you like, bathing as much as you like, if dissatisfaction arises in you and passion assails your heart, then emit semen using your hand."
>
> "But, your reverence, are you sure that it is suitable to act like this ?"
>
> "Yes, your reverence, I do this."
>
> Then the venerable Seyyasaka ate as much as he liked, slept as much as he liked, bathed as much as he liked; but having eaten as much as he liked, slept as much as he liked, bathed as much as he liked, dissatisfaction arose, and passion assailed his heart, so he emitted semen using his hand. Then in a short time the venerable Seyyasaka was nice looking with rounded features, of a bright complexion and a clear skin.

So the monks who were the friends of the venerable Seyyasaka spoke thus to the venerable Seyyasaka :

"Formerly, reverend Seyyasaka, you were thin, wretched, of a bad color, yellowish, with the veins showing all over your body. But now, at present, you are nice looking with rounded features, of a bright complexion and a clear skin. Why now, do you take medicine, reverend Seyyasaka ?"

"I do not take medicine, your reverences, but I am eating as much as I like, I am sleeping as much as I like, I am bathing as much as I like; then eating as much as I like, sleeping as much as I like, bathing as much as I like, if dissatisfaction arises in me and passion assails the heart, I emit semen using my hand."

"But do you, reverend Seyyasaka, eat the gifts of faith with the very same hand as that which you use to emit semen ?"

"Yes, your reverences," he said.

Those who were modest monks became annoyed, vexed and angry saying :

"How can the venerable Seyyasaka emit semen in this way ?"

Then these monks, having rebuked the venerable Seyyasaka in various ways, told this matter to the lord. Then the lord on this occasion, in this connection, having had the order of monks convened, asked the venerable Seyyasaka :

"Is it true, as is said, that you, Seyyasaka, using your hand, emit semen ?"

"It is true, lord," he said.

The enlightened one, the lord, rebuked him, saying :

"It is not fit, foolish man, it is not becoming, it is not suitable, it is not worthy of a recluse, it is not right, it is not to be done. How can you, foolish man, emit semen using your hand ? Foolish man, have I not uttered dhamma in many ways for the stilling of passion, and not for the sake of passion, taught dhamma for the sake of being devoid of the fetters, and not for the sake of being bound, taught dhamma for the sake of being without grasping, and not for the sake of grasping ? How can you, foolish man, while dhamma is taught by me for the sake of passionlessness, strive after passion ? How can you, while dhamma is taught for the sake of being devoid of the fetters, strive after being bound ? How can you, while dhamma is taught for the sake of being without grasping strive after grasping ? Foolish man, have I not taught dhamma in various ways for the stilling of passion, taught dhamma for the subduing of conceit, for the restraint of thirst, for the elimination of attachment, for the cutting through the round of becomings, for the destruction of craving, for passionlessness, for stopping, for waning ? Foolish man, have I not declared in various ways the destruction of the pleasures of the senses, declared the full understanding of ideas of the pleasures of the senses, declared the restraint of the thirst for pleasures of the senses, declared the elimination of thoughts of pleasures of the senses, declared the allaying of the fever of pleasures of the senses ? Foolish man, it is not for the benefit of unbelievers, nor for increase in the number of believers, but it is, foolish man, to the detriment of unbelievers as well as of believers, and it causes wavering in some."

Then the lord having rebuked the venerable Seyyasaka in various ways on account of his difficulty in maintaining his state... said :

"... Thus, monks, this course of training should be set forth:

Intentional emission of semen is a matter entailing a formal meeting of the Order."

Thus this course of training for monks was made known to the lord.

Now at that time, monks, having eaten abundant food, went to sleep, thoughtless and careless. While they were sleeping, thoughtless and careless, one of them emitted semen as the result of a dream. These were remorseful and said : "The course of training made known by the lord says that intentional emission of semen is a matter requiring a formal meeting of the Order; and because of a dream one of us (did this). Now is this intention permitted ? What now if we have fallen into an offence requiring a formal meeting of the Order ?" They told this matter to the lord. He said :

"Monks, this was the intention, but it does not apply. Monks, this course of training should be set forth :

Intentional emission of semen except during a dream is an offence requiring a formal meeting of the Order."[1]

Saṅghādisesa I contains many of the issues that will provide us with grist for further discussion in the next chapter. But for

1. *Book of Discipline* 1 : 193-196.

now, we will confine our remarks to the key factor involved in the making of legal decisions in Buddhist law.

We want to call attention to the fact that the Buddha's initial promulgation had to be amended in light of the ambiguous circumstances related in the second story. Though the text attributes the reformulation of the rule to the Buddha, it is highly likely that it is a specimen of "monkish labor" at work. Or if you will, a matter arose within the *bhikkhu* community requiring a refinement of the Buddha's initial proclamation. The immediate task at hand was to determine the applicability of the rule, to be consistent with the understood intention of the law. If *bhikkhus* emit semen when they do not intend to, they are not held to be guilty of transgressing the rule. Thus, while two different *bhikkhus* may discharge semen, the same action can be judged as either an infraction against the rules of discipline or merely as an unintentional accident that bears no blame. The issue at stake is not emitting semen, but the condition of one's volition that can give rise to such a bodily expression. This same principle is operative consistently throughout *Suttavibhaṅga* literature. For example, in one story that occurs in connection with the *pārājika* injunction concerned with not taking human life, a *bhikkhu* is judged not guilty if he accidentally drops an object from above killing someone down below.[1] There are many stories involving the Chabbaggiyas, six monks who continually seek ways to confound the law, in which judgments according to intention are specifically applied. A particularly graphic example of the importance of intention is evident in a tale about a *bhikkhu* who engages a female monkey in sexual intercourse and proceeds to argue his innocence on the basis that the rule against sexual intercourse applies only to intercourse with human beings. As a result, the rule is amended so that all types of intercourse are prohibited.[2] And, more importantly, the *bhikkhu* in question is found guilty because he has not stilled his passions. Here, again, emphasis is placed upon the disposition that gave rise to the act in question. And, it is upon the evaluation of that disposition that the appropriate judgment is rendered. (In a later discussion concerned with the *Pavāraṇā* ritual, we shall see exactly how this determination was worked out in formal

1. *Book of Discipline* 1: 138.
2. Ibid., 1 : 38-40.

fashion.) But the important point to be made here is that Buddhist law is more concerned with fulfilling the intent or "spirit" of the law than it is concerned with abiding by the literal letter of the law. Consequently, emphasis is placed not so much upon the fact that the Buddha laid down such and such a precept to be followed uncritically, but rather upon the fact that the disciplinary rules facilitate a mind-set conducive to the norms of *Dhamma.* Transgressing the rules is understood to be evidence of an undisciplined disposition. Although the letter of the law may be fulfilled, e.g., the *bhikkhu* in question in the last example had not committed sexual intercourse with a human being, the spirit of the law had been violated.[1]

Therefore, even though the Buddha can be understood as functioning in the same manner as a sovereign authority, his role in that capacity does not provide us grounds to argue that Buddhist law represents the type of positive law that Austin argues for. The validity of Buddhist law does not abide ultimately in the fact that the law is commanded by sovereignty. Rather, its validity and applicability rest upon consistency with a higher norm conducive to realizing the soteriological goal.

The question that we must now answer is this : what constitutes this norm upon which the disciplinary rules are based and interpreted ? And, what is the ethos of the norm ?

In pondering these questions, we are led to consider the

1. The very same type of argument has been used against Austin's claims that law is legitimate because of the fact that it has been laid down by unquestioned authority. Ronald Dworkin cites an 1889 case settled by the New York Court of Appeals in which the court had to decide whether an heir named in his grandfather's will could inherit under that will, even though he had murdered his grandfather. The court began its reasoning in this way : "It is quite true that statutes regulating the making, proof, and effect of wills, and the devolution of property, if literally construed, and if their force and effect can in no way and under no circumstances be controlled or modified, give property to this murderer." But continuing, "all laws as well as all contracts may be controlled in their operation and effect by general, fundamental maxims of common law. No one shall be permitted to profit by his own fraud, or to take advantage of his own wrong, or to found any claim upon his own iniquity, or to acquire property by his own crime." The murderer did not receive what he had thought was his due inheritance. The spirit of the law had been violated. Conforming to the law rests upon the nature of one's intent. Ronald Dworkin, "The Model of Rules," in Feinberg, ed. *Philosophy of Law*, pp. 74-92.

fundamental relationship that exists between morality and legality. From one perspective, law may be seen as an instrument to administer morality. In this view, morality is constitutive of the norm that we have referred to. And, by again returning to the *Vinaya* and by appealing to other early Buddhist canonical texts, we find some justification for arguing that morality is the issue which is at the heart of the Buddhist disciplinary code.

The Buddhist notion of morality is an exceedingly rich concept that has enjoyed widespread discussion in early Buddhist texts. Generally, the term *sīla* designates virtuous behavior, ethical conduct, or the living of a moral life. As we noted in our introduction, the Buddha's solution to man's problematic existence lies in his Noble Eightfold Path formula, a formula that rests upon the three elemental conceptions of *sīla*, *samādhi* (concentration, meditation) and *paññā* (wisdom). *Sīla* is the aspect of the religious life to be cultivated in terms of right conduct, right speech and right livelihood. *Sīla* is often understood to be the first necessary step that a *bhikkhu* must realize in his path to attaining *nibbāna*. *Suttas* such as the *Sāmaññaphala Suttanta* of the *Dīgha Nikāya* list *sīla* as the initial point of departure. However, we must also keep in mind that the spiritual pursuit of the *bhikkhu* is fundamentally an integration of *sīla*, *samādhi* and *paññā*. H. Saddhatissa, in his fine treatment of Buddhist ethics, writes that

> Clearly the components of the Noble Eightfold path are not to be counted as consecutive steps, but even though one takes Right Speech, Right Action and Right Livelihood components of the *Sīla* group first, in accordance with the order of the three sections *Sīla*, *Samādhi* and *Paññā*, one remarks immediately that neither Right Speech nor Right Action, much less Right Livelihood, is possible without Right Understanding. The interrelation of the components is inevitable, and recognizing this one comes again to the strength of the Buddhist teaching, namely that Moralities are never an end in themselves; they are inextricably bound up with all the other components which form the path to final release from suffering.[1]

Saddhatissa's remarks underscore the fact that the integrated

1. H. Saddhatissa, *Buddhist Ethics* (London : George Allen and Unwin, Ltd., 1970), p. 74.

position of *sīla* is evident throughout the Pāli Canon. The four cardinal precepts of morality that make up the *pārājika* section of the disciplinary rules appear in no less than sixteen *suttas* of the *Dīgha* and *Majjhima Nikāyas*. Observance of the *pārājikas* is said to be relevant to every type of spiritual attainment ranging from the acquisition of mystical and magical powers (*iddhi*) to becoming the best of teachers.[1] Before we attempt to discern the relationship between morality and the many rules constitutive of the disciplinary code, we need to review the importance attached to *sīla* in several of these *suttas*. Therein, we can see how the *pārājikas*, which form the heart of *sīla* concerns, can be viewed from one perspective as constitutive of a moral norm upon which many of the disciplinary rules are based.

We have already mentioned the *Aggañña Sutta* in connection with our discussion of viewing the figure of the Buddha in relation to royal imagery. But the heart of that *sutta* is reflected in a phrase that occurs no less than eight times :

For the norm [dhamma] is the best among this folk,
Both in this world and the next.[2]

Essentially, the significance of this refrain is found within the context of the central argument of the text : that the various stratifications of society are due to the realization of *Dhamma* or adhering to the norm, rather than being the consequence of heredity or bloodlines. The Buddhist argument is that an individual's place in society is determined by conformity to the moral law of the cosmos. As the *sutta* progresses, decay of moral standards leads to the necessity of contracting a king to enforce order. Moral decline begins with the introductión of greedy disposition[3] and the recognition of individuality which feeds upon craving. Lust, stealing and lying result and adherence to the norm is forsaken. With the innovation of kingship, we are given the origins of the *khattiya* class. The origins of the *brahmins*, *vessas*, and *suddas* are then recounted according to the well-known societal functions they perform. But in each case, their destinies at death are said to be determined on the basis of how they lived their lives as expressed through deeds of thought,

1. T. W. Rhys Davids, Introduction to "Samañña-phala Sutta," *Dialogues of the Buddha* 1 : 57-59.
2. *Dialogues of the Buddha*, 3 : 80-94.
3. Ibid., pp. 82-83.

word and bodily expression. Thus, it is the moral law of *kammic* retribution that determines rebirth status. Over against the four classes of society, another figure is introduced who has put away all evils by destroying the cankers. And this new figure who has perfected the norm is the *arahan*, "chief among them, in virtue of the norm, not in absence of the norm."[1] The apology concludes. Succinctly put, the argument contained in this *sutta* amounts to an appeal that men be evaluated not according to the bloodlines of birth, but according to the worthiness of their actions measured against the norm of *Dhamma*.

In the *Aggañña Sutta*, we have already been given a hint as to what consists of the norm. As lust, lying and stealing are generated out of greed and craving, which lead to chaos and decline, abstaining from these actions in body, speech and thought presumably leads to a favorable rebirth, or, in the case of an *arahan*, to transcending the realm of continuous becoming. But in the *Cakkavatti-Sihanada Suttanta*,[2] there is an even clearer depiction of the norm. In this rich mythology, the Buddha, in the opening lines, urges his *bhikkhus* to live as "islands unto themselves" taking refuge in the norm (Dhamma).[3] He then proceeds to tell the tale of *cakkavattis* and their endeavors to maintain the law. The *cakkavatti* (literally : wheel-turner) conquers the four quarters of the universe by means of righteousness rather than by force. When rival kings ask to be taught the essential nature of the power which enables the *cakkavatti* to keep the Wheel of Law in motion, the reply is as follows :

> Slay no living thing. Take not that which has not been given. Do not act wrongly by touching bodily desires. Speak no lies. Drink no intoxicants.[4]

Bringing all rivals under rule by means of righteousness, the *cakkavattis* of this *sutta* became paradigmatic for Buddhist kings throughout the history of the tradition. But of more importance to our discussion is the fact that the norm of *Dhamma* which constitutes righteousness is identical to the concerns of the *brāhmaṇical pañcaśila*, the significance of which is to be discerned shortly. The rest of the *sutta* describes how moral decay sets in when kings

1. *Dialogues of the Buddha*, 3: 93.
2. Ibid., pp. 59-76.
3. Ibid., p. 59.
4. Ibid., pp. 63-64.

neglect their duties to keep the Wheel of Law in motion. Killing, stealing, lying and sexual misconduct emerge in the world as the norm becomes further neglected. The life spans of human beings become gradually shorter until the appearance of a future king who will re-establish the norm in preparation for the coming of the next Buddha, Metteyya. The *sutta* ends with a description of the *bhikkhu* who realizes the norm and in so doing ultimately achieves *arahan*ship. Yet, the cultivation of moral (*sīla*) conduct, i.e., adherence to the *pañcaśīla* (essentially the same concerns expressed in the *Vinaya*'s four *pārājikas*), is considered to be only a prerequisite to attaining the final goal. Nevertheless, since the *pañcaśīla* (the norm of *Dhamma* maintained by the *cakkavatti*) corresponds to the concerns of the *pārājikas* of the *Vinaya*, we have located a clear connection between the righteous morality which is the norm of *Dhamma* and the most mportant disciplinary rules.

This connection is reinforced when we observe how the nature of morality is treated in the *Sigālovāda Suttanta* of the *Dīgha Nikāya*. In his commentary on this *sutta*, Buddhaghoṣa says "nothing in the duties of the houseman is left unmentioned. This Suttanta is called the Vinaya of the Houseman. Hence, in one who practices what has been taught in it, growth is to be looked for, and not decay."[1] Buddhaghoṣa's comment is telling : he attributes to this homily the same importance that is indicative of the *bhikkhu Vinaya*; in fact, he has gone so far as to call the moral exhortations of this *sutta* constitutive of *Vinaya*. And when we read from the opening lines of this homily, we see that there are good reasons for Buddhaghoṣa to regard this *sutta* in such fashion : as the *pārājikas* serve as the initial concern of the *bhikkhu Vinaya*, so too are they identified with great importance in the opening lines of the *Sigāla* homily :

> Inasmuch, young householder, as the Arian disciple has put away the four vices of conduct, inasmuch as he does no evil actions from the four motives,[2] inasmuch as he does not

1. Cited in Rhys Davids, Introduction to the "Sigālovāda Suttanta," *Dialogues of the Buddha* 3 : 169.

2. Here the motivation of "fear" is added to "passion, hatred and delusion," the three motivations or "wrongful states of mind" identified in the *Vinaya* as generating undisciplined actions. The great importance attached to eradicating these states of mind will be addressed in the following chapter.

pursue the six channels for dissipating wealth, he thus, in avoiding the fourteen evil things is a coverer of the six quarters; he has practiced so as to conquer both worlds; he tastes success in this world and the next. At the dissolution of the body, he is reborn to a happy destiny in heaven. What are the four vices of conduct he has put away ? The destruction of life, the taking of what is not given, licentiousness, and lying speech. These are the four vices of conduct that he has put away.[1]

Abstaining from the four vices, i.e., the *Vinaya*'s *pārājikas*, results in harmonious relations among the laity. And on the level of soteriology, the practice of virtue is held to be superior to the worshiping of deities. Morality allows one to be a conqueror of the "six quarters."[2] Favorable rebirth is the consequence. As the *bhikkhu Vinaya* needs to be cultivated for a *bhikkhu* to progress along the path to *nibbāna*, so too does adherence of the "householder's *Vinaya*" enable the layman to achieve his goal of favorable rebirth.

Thus, a case can be made for the concerns of *sīla* being constitutive of the norm upon which discipline is based. And this is precisely the line of argument assumed by one modern academic in his exposition on the *Vinaya* rules.

W. Pachow believes that the Buddhist disciplinary code is fundamentally an elaboration of *pañcaśīla*. He observes that many of the minor rules of discipline may have been motivated out of the concerns expressed in the *pārājikas* about the taking of life, stealing, lying and sexual misconduct. In order to prove his point, he categorizes the many minor rules of discipline in such a way as to show their relationships to one of the major precepts that make up the *pārājika* section of the disciplinary code. Having done so, he goes on to say that

> It would not be unreasonable to say that the code of discipline is but an enlarged edition of the Pañcaśīla which have been adopted by the Buddhists and Jainas from the Brāhmaṇical ascetics. And under various circumstances, they have developed subsidiary rules in order to meet various requirements on

1. *Dialogues of the Buddha* 3 : 174.
2. This is an allusion to the practice of worshiping the *brāhmaṇical* deities Agni, Indra, Varuṇa, Soma, Viṣṇu and Bṛhaspati. The point here is that the practice of *sīla* is a more auspicious spiritual endeavor than the worship of these *vedic* gods.

various occasions [sic]. This appears to be the line of development through which the growth of these rules could be explained.[1]

Pachow's contention is well worth considering in our attempt to find a basis for Buddhist discipline. In the first instance he has tried to show a fundamental relationship between the major concerns of *sīla*, i.e., taking life, stealing, lying, and sexual misconduct, and the many secondary rules making up the disciplinary code. If these many minor rules are but extensions of the more major, the minor rules can be viewed as forming a type of preventive defense. That is, for example, since there are over fifty minor rules that in some way restrict a *bhikkhu*'s behavior around women, we can understand the motivations for such restrictions as being rooted in the first *pārājika* which prohibits sexual intercourse. The same principle applies to the other three *pārājikas* as well. We have attempted to demonstrate just how many of the minor rules can be linked to major rules in charts to be found below in Appendix I. In tabulating our results, we have been even more liberal in our associations than Pachow was in his effort.[2] For example, when a *bhikkhu* is required to wear a waist cloth "even all around" as he is required to do in the first *sekhiya*, or generally, to keep a proper appearance (which is the issue at stake in the first twenty-six *sekhiyas*) we have categorized these rules as extensions of the first *pārājika* which prohibits sexual intercourse. By giving such scrutiny to the body, bodily excitement can be prevented or carefully monitored. By using this kind of tabular analysis, 139 out of the 227 Pāli disciplinary rules enumerated in the *Suttavibhaṅga* can be accounted for. But eighty-eight rules remain outstanding. Pachow encountered the same problem in his analysis. The way in which he accounted for the rules which he could not accommodate according to his schema was to generate additional categories : (1) "rules relating to food, drink, medicine, etc."; (2) "rules relating to robes, bowls, rugs, bedding, etc."; (3) "rules relating to housing, staying, association, bathing and comfort, etc."; and (4) "rules relating to trade, digging, wandering, touching money and treasures, etc."[3]

1. W. Pachow, *A Comparative Study of the Pratimokṣa* (Santiniketan, India : Sino-Indian Cultural Society, 1955), p. 37.
2. See Appendix, pp. 145-146.
3. Pachow, *A Comparative Study*, Appendix I, pp. 1-2.

Is this type of analysis of the disciplinary rules adequate ? Is it convincing to argue that *sīla* is the root concept lying behind the formulation of the disciplinary code ? Is *sīla* that which is legislated in Buddhist law ?

If this hypothesis were absolutely sound, we could somehow relate all of the disciplinary rules in some way to the four *pārājikas* or to the *pañcaśīla*. Unfortunately, we are not able to do this. In fact, Pachow found it necessary to generate additional categories to account for the remaining rules that do not seem to be derived from *sīla* concerns. That necessity would appear to contradict his thesis. Perhaps part of the problem could be solved if the *sekhiyas* were not considered as part of the original disciplinary code, an issue we have referred to earlier. Yet, we would then have to ask the question : on what basis were the *sekhiyas* later found to be constitutive of discipline ? And this is but the first of several problems we encounter if we rest content with the hypothesis that morality is the comprehensive norm upon which the Buddhist disciplinary rules are based.

The most fundamental problem with this perspective is that it in no way accounts for the particular genius of the disciplinary rules. As we noted in a passing reference to the *Samañña-phala Suttanta*, the four *pārājikas* are listed among the moralities which constitute one of thirteen perfections gained by the ardent recluse. But Rhys Davids points out that all but one of these perfections, or "fruits of the life of a recluse," cannot be considered as essentially Buddhistic; but rather twelve of these perfections, including the moralities, were characteristic of many other contemporary heterodox groups as well.[1] This problem is expanded by two other considerations. The first has already been noted by Pachow : the *pañcaśīla* were also observed the *brāhmaṇ*ical ascetics. This means that *sīla* need not be considered as even particularly *śramaṇ*ic. The second observation compounding the problem becomes apparent when we remember that the four

1. T. W. Rhys Davids, Introduction to the "Samañña," p. 63. Significantly, the one factor that Rhys Davids holds is particularly Buddhistic is the realization of the Four Noble Truths, the last of the thirteen enumerated perfections. Thus, our own endeavors in the next chapter to discern a Buddhistic basis for the disciplinary rules must be rooted, therefore, in a consideration of the importance of realizing the veracity of the Four Noble Truths. That is, we must determine how realization of the Four Noble Truths relates to the practice of Buddhist discipline.

pārājikas also show up prominently in the *Sigāla* homily which outlines morality for the laity. Thus, if we are to argue that the fundamental basis of Buddhist discipline consists of the primary concerns of *sīla*, we would have to admit that the basis of Buddhist discipline is not exclusively Buddhistic, nor *śramaṇic*, nor even monastic for that matter : not a very satisfying finding.

Finally, there is a crucial problem encountered when we attempt to relate this thesis to soteriology. Since both laity and *bhikkhus* observe the same morality, why is it that the soteriological consequences vary : *nibbāna* for the *bhikkhu* and a more favorable rebirth for the laity ? Is it the case that performing the same moral deeds, or abstaining from committing prohibited actions, results in different consequences ?

In short, by considering the primary concerns of *sīla* as they are reflected in the *pārājikas*, we are unable to mount a convincing argument that identifies the undergirding principle of Buddhist discipline. This is not to deny that *sīla* plays a very important role. At least one school of Buddhism considered the recitation of the disciplinary rules to be a proclamation of the community's "pure *sīla*."[1] However, the disciplinary code must be understood in a broader context than merely as an extension of *sīla*, one of the primary elements of the Noble Eightfold Path. We must recognize discipline as a reflection of one who has come to realize the veracity of the Four Noble Truths in their entirety.

In our consideration of how Buddhist law was interpreted and applied, we noted the great importance attached to the state of a *bhikkhu*'s disposition. Discipline is therefore more than adhering to a general moral norm. Rather, it consists of being completely aware of the nature of one's actions. That is to say, mindfulness and concentration are intricately involved in the process of discipline. A disciplined action is more than just the avoidance of killing, lying, stealing, and sexual misconduct. It is the effective expression of one who has been converted to a way of looking at the world, one who has embraced the perspective and world view realized by the Buddha and expounded in his central teachings. In the next chapter, we must view discipline within that context.

1. The Mahāsāṃghikas.

CHAPTER FIVE

THE STRUCTURE OF DISCIPLINED ACTIONS

We have now arrived at a critical juncture in our discussion of Buddhist discipline and can proceed to the heart of our analysis. In this chapter, we shall develop a new model for understanding Buddhist discipline that is not dependent upon an understanding of the *Vinaya* precepts in terms of moral law enforced by sovereign authority or as an elaboration of the concerns of *sīla*. Rather, we want to look at the very structure of Buddhist action as it is understood within the context of the *Suttavibhaṅga* and other canonical sources. In determining this structure, we shall see that although the *Suttavibhaṅga* formulations may appear to be complex and irregular at first sight, all of them are grounded in a definite pattern of scholastic logic which is guided by the soteriological concerns of the Four Noble Truths.

In the previous chapter, we noted the pre-eminent concern given to the factor of intention or volition in determining the rights and wrongs of *bhikkhu* behavior. The importance of intention or volition is not limited to ethical questions or to juridical hermeneutics, but lies at the basis of Buddhist discipline and consequently, at the basis of soteriological achievement. I. B. Horner, in the conclusion to her *Early Buddhist Theory of Man Perfected*, sums up her findings by saying:

> Implicit in the notion of crossing over the flood is the idea of crossing it by means of the choosing will. The choice of the man or woman who wills is based on right knowledge and this is based on the desire to know aright and its fulfilment. Such desire and realization are possible only after the mind has been cleansed of the cloying and hankering desire for pleasure and sensations. Thus it is that the will, in common with all those determinations towards asceticism, rightly understood, may be directed to choose, in preference to the lower, the development of the higher, which is the Way of arahanship.[1]

Horner's emphasis upon the importance of the will also takes into account the significance of knowledge. Right knowledge is

1. Horner, *Early Buddhist Theory*, pp. 280-281.

understood to be a prerequisite for a properly choosing will. One does not will to act in a disciplined manner because an external standard is being enforced. Instead, one wills to act because his actions are in conformity with his own inward state that has been cultured by awareness derived from right knowledge. We must therefore raise the question: what constitutes this right knowledge?

To answer this question requires returning to the *Vinaya*. Although we are primarily concerned with the nature of Buddhist action as it can be derived in the *Suttavibhaṅga*, the first chapter of the *Mahāvagga* contains a pattern of events of great significance to our discussion. The initial chapter of the *Mahāvagga* recounts the origins of the Buddhist community. In this account, after the Buddha has achieved enlightenment, he embarks upon his missionary career triumphantly converting those who are willing to listen to his message. In these conversion stories, we can note that two different types of interchange occur whenever the Buddha encounters a prospective convert. The first type of interchange is indicative of what it means to become a lay convert while the second is a depiction of what is entailed in becoming a *bhikkhu*.

In the interchanges of the first type, Gotama meets a prospective convert and preaches a sermon whereby

> the Lord talked a progressive talk . . . that is to say, talk on giving, talk on moral habit, talk on heaven, he explained the vanity, depravity of pleasures of the senses, the advantage of renouncing them.[1]

Upon hearing this sermon, the listener takes refuge in the Buddha, the *Dhamma* and the *Saṅgha* and becomes a lay adherent. The elements of this sermon reflect the central aspects of religious piety to be cultivated in the lay life. Emphasis is placed upon the positive *kamm*ic efficacy resulting from giving (*dāna*)[2] and moral rectitude, while a warning is issued about the pitfalls in store for those who act without reckoning with desire. In accordance with a life lived in virtue, the individual can expect to reap the fruit of good actions by being reborn in heaven.

1. This stock phrase occurs first in *Book of Discipline* 4 : 23 and is repeated at least eight times in the Mahāvagga account. It also appears in connection with other conversion events recounted in the *Nikāyas*. See Horner's note in *Book of Discipline* 4 : 23, n. 1 for further textual references.

2. The reference to "giving" refers to providing the *bhikkhusaṅgha* with need material requisites, a fortuitous merit-making act.

Tachibana, in his *Ethics of Buddhism*, has observed that the motives which govern virtuous actions in the lay religious life correspond on the cosmological level with the grades of heavenly rebirth to be won by ardent lay devotees. He argues that

> since there are, according to Buddhist cosmology, five spheres of heavenly world between the Catummahārājika and the Brahmankāyika, it seems that these motives are arranged according to the value of rewards which these seven will bring in the next world.[1]

Tachibana discerns a direct causal relationship between the quality of one's motives and soteriological achievement. It must be emphasized that the will, directed by one's motives, is the key factor involved that gives rise to the cosmological result. We are beginning to understand why so much emphasis is placed on volition or motivation in the *Suttavibhaṅga*'s interpretations of the applicability of disciplinary precepts. Yet, we are still confronted with the problem which was raised towards the end of the last chapter, namely, what allows for *bhikkhu* actions to be considered so much more fortuitous ?

By considering the second type of interchange that occurs in the conversion accounts described in the *Mahāvagga*, we can offer a solution to this problem. The second kind of interchange begins in the same manner as the first with the preaching of the sermon cited above. However, if the Buddha perceives that the prospective convert has a mind capable of understanding further,[2] if the prospect's mind is "devoid of hindrances," a second sermon is preached. This second sermon is the same as the Buddha's famous Deer Park homily containing the Four Noble Truths. When the listener hears this sermon, he gains *Dhamma*-vision or the *Dhamma*-Eye. *Dhamma*-vision refers to a grasping of the "principal doctrine of the Buddhas" or the meaning of the teaching :

> When this is present, that comes to be;
> from the arising of this, that arises.

1. S. Tachibana, *The Ethics of Buddhism* (London : Oxford University Press, 1926), pp. 207-208. Cf. *Book of Gradual Sayings* 1:190, wherein these motives (faith, virtue, religious knowledge, liberality and personal insight) are discussed in relation to heavenly rebirth.

2. Here we have references to the skilful means (*upāya*) attributed to the Buddha by the Mahāyāna traditions.

When this is absent, that does not come to be :
of the cessation of this, that ceases.[1]

Having come to this realization, the prospective convert takes refuge and joins the *bhikkhusangha.* He has been converted to a new paradigm of understanding existence and embraces a new world view that will affect his judgment, motivations and consequently his actions. What the *bhikkhu* convert gains is an awareness of co-dependent arising (*paṭiccasamuppāda*). It is an awareness of the conditioned and causal nature of existence. By knowing the interrelationality of all that is, he can act accordingly to determine his spiritual fate.

The fundamental significance of this awareness lies at the heart of the Noble Eightfold Path that leads to *nibbāna.*[2] In explicating his claim as to the centrality of mindfulness, Rhys Davids notes that it is mindfulness of *paṭiccasamuppāda* that is most crucial :

> What then is Mindfulness ? . . . Etymologically Sati is Memory. But as happened at the rise of Buddhism to so many other expressions in common use, a new connotation was then attached to the word, a connotation that gave a new meaning to it, and renders 'memory' a most inadequate and misleading translation. It became memory, recollection, calling-to-mind, being aware of, certain specified facts. Of these, the most important was the impermanence (the coming to be as the result of a cause, and the passing away again of all phenomena, bodily and mental). And it included the repeated application of this awareness, to each experience of life. . .[3]

In the introductory chapter, we noted that the suffering which man experiences is due the way in which he perceives existence. That is, by mistakenly taking the impermanent to be real, one regards one's own being as a concrete independent entity. This results in the sense of *ahaṃkāra* and the production of a state of mind which fosters craving. Awareness of the conditioned nature of existence allows one to prevent ego-consciousness from assailing

1. *Book of Discipline* 4 : 23.
2. Rhys Davids, Introduction to the "Mahāsatipatthana Suttanta," *Dialogues of the Buddha* 3 : 322. Cf. Saddhatissa, *Buddhist Ethics*, p. 28 and Tachibana, *Ethics* , pp. 106-107.
3. Rhys Davids, Introduction to the "Mahāsatipatthana Suttanta," p. 322.

perception. One who has the *Dhamma*-Eye can become detached, or can remove the conditions which give rise to false perception. That is to say, elimination of ego-consciousness changes the normal process of perception. With the attainment of this awareness, one is able to prevent the influx of impure "wrongful" states of mind such as passion, hatred and delusion which texture the mind so as to give rise to attached actions which require *kamm*ic retribution. An enlightened one's perception remains untainted when in contact with the phenomenal world. Such an individual remains secure and at peace in the midst of all of the destruction and confusion in this world. As Kalupahana puts it :

> This form of behavior is described as "going against the current." It is called "going against the stream" because, unlike the ordinary man, the person who has attained emancipation does not allow any attachment to arise in him when he perceives a pleasurable object, even though he experiences a pleasurable feeling. Hence, for him there is no grasping.[1]

What separates the laity from the *bhikkhus* in this case, then, is the fact that *bhikkhus* are considered to be more acutely aware of the causal nature of existence. They are said to be possessors of the *Dhamma*-Eye, a facility that allows them insight into what must be accomplished to reach the higher goal. Awareness derived from the knowledge of *paṭiccasamuppāda* textures their disposition or provides what we will now begin calling disciplined disposition, a controlled will which generates actions transcending the determination of *kamm*ic retribution as they normally apply.

Now, in returning to the *Suttavibhaṅga,* we can determine how all of this bears directly on an understanding of the basis of Buddhist discipline. And, it is more than fitting that we begin to see connections in the opening story that commences the *Suttavibhaṅga*'s treatment of the disciplinary rules.

The *Suttavibhaṅga* begins under the heading of the first *pārājika*, the cardinal precept which prohibits sexual misconduct. In our description of the way in which a precept is presented, we noted that a story or stories serve(s) as a type of case history leading up to the rule's proclamation. In the case of the first *pārājika*, there are seven such stories presented before the final formulation of the rule is given. And upon closer scrutiny, we find that only

1. Kalupahana, *Causality*, pp. 139-140.

the last three stories have a direct bearing upon *pārājika* I. The first four stories serve as an introduction to the entire *Vinaya*. By far, the most important of these stories is the very first,[1] for within this story the Buddha is engaged in a discourse wherein he explicitly describes the nature of a disciplined action. By analyzing the details of this discourse, we shall be able to construct a framework in which to classify and interpret the entire disciplinary code.

The initial two pages of the *Suttavibhaṅga* are dedicated to a description of the Buddha as "fully enlightened, perfected, endowed with knowledge and conduct."[2] Gotama is thus the Buddha because he has experienced the truth, and, the teachings that follow represent a means by which the truth can be realized by all who have the right resolve. After the description of the Buddha as the Tathāgata, the Buddha encounters a certain *brahmin* of Verañja who makes a number of observations about the Buddha's teachings. These observations elicit responses from the Buddha which indicate the special significance of discipline. We shall now be preoccupied by these responses.

The first observation that the *brahmin* offers is a contention that the Buddha is not respectful to old *brahmins* because he does not properly greet them and ask them to sit down. The Buddha replies that a *tathāgata* is not required to greet or rise up for any

1. As we shall focus upon the very first story of the *Suttavibhaṅga*, we shall here very briefly mention the concerns of the second, third and fourth stories. The primary motif of the second story (*Book of Discipline*, 1 : 11-14) is concerned with the rationale for the practice of alms rounds : since food can be obtained in this manner, *bhikkhus* will not engage in the practice of cultivating the soil; therefore, they avoid doing harm to any creatures that dwell therein. The third story is a very important tale that explains why the *Pāṭimokkha* has been laid down. We find the definitive sentence : "Hence, the teacher makes known the course of training, and appoints the Pātimokkha in order to ward off those conditions causing the cankers." Ibid., p. 19. In the following pages, we shall have occasion for indicating the significance of this phrase for the understanding of *bhikkhu* discipline. The fourth story contains a legend wherein the lay practice of providing *bhikkhus* with housing and provisions during the rainy season and robes at its conclusion is established. Ibid., pp. 20-21. There is no doubt that this legend is placed at the beginning of the *Vinaya* in order to establish the authoritative origins of the *Kaṭhina* rite and the practice of *vassa*. We shall have more to say about the *Kaṭhina* ritual in a following chapter.

2. *Book of Discipline* 1 : 1-2.

creature in the universe. That response indicates the pre-eminent status gained by the Buddha. But the second observation offered by the *brahmin*, like all of the observations that follow, is directed in a straightforward way to the Buddha's central teachings. The *brahmin* asserts that "the revered Gotama is without the quality of taste." In reply, the Buddha answers in a stock manner that characterizes the remaining exchanges during the story :

> There is indeed, brahmin, a way in which one speaking truly of me could say : The recluse Gotama is without the quality of taste. For, brahmin, tastes for forms, tastes for sounds, tastes for scents, tastes for savours, tastes for tangible objects—these have been destroyed by the Tathāgata, cut off at the root like a palm-tree, they are so utterly done away with that they are not able to come into future existence. This, brahmin, is a way in which one speaking truly of me could say : The recluse Gotama is without the quality of taste. But surely you did not mean that.[1]

All of the remaining responses contain the phrase "There is a way in which one speaking truly of me could say : "The recluse Gotama is . . ." and "But surely you did not mean that." Those two phrases signify a very important and fundamental fact for the Buddha : the *brahmin*, or anyone else who has not heard the Four Noble Truths cannot possibly understand the meaning of the Buddha's teaching. Such a person is still confounded by his condition of ignorance (*avijjā*) and thus misses the true significance of what the Buddha has taught. Indeed, the *Saṃyutta Nikāya* (II.4) defines ignorance precisely in terms of lack of knowledge of the Four Noble Truths :

> By ignorance is meant lack of knowledge with regard to the unsatisfactoriness of things, lack of knowledge with regard to the cause of unsatisfactoriness, lack of knowledge with regard to the cessation of this sense of unsatisfactoriness, and lack of knowledge with regard to the path leading to this cessation.[2]

Because the *brahmin* is ignorant, the Buddha may conclude his response by saying : "But surely you did not mean that." In every response that the Buddha gives to the *brahmin*, the Buddha's answer is framed within those two phrases that signify the brahmin's ignorance.

1. *Book of Discipline* 1 : 3.
2. *Book of Kindred Sayings* 2 : 4-5.

But the Buddha's response is packed with meaning in another regard. When the Buddha says that he has no taste for forms, sounds, scents, savours, and tangible objects, he is saying that he exercises self-restraint over his sense organs which include the eye, the ear, the nose, the tongue, the body and the mind. A passage from the *Aṅguttara Nikāya* highlights the importance of restraining the sense organs :

> Here, O monks, is a monk who sees with the eye, but is not affected by its features and minor characteristics. If [he is affected by them] and lives without controlling his organ of vision, as a result, covetousness, dejection, and sinful evil things will befall him. But he takes steps for its control; he keeps watch on his organ of vision, and brings it into perfect control.[1]

The same is then repeated about the five other sense organs. Here we have an explicit reference to the importance of being totally aware of stimuli that are received through the sense organs. The point of keeping vigilance over the senses is not to block out the stimuli received through them, but rather to recognize these stimuli and then control the effect they have on one's disposition. Tachibana has suggested that we understand the sense organs as "doors" through which stimuli are received.[2] Within the Buddha's formulation, the reception of stimuli designates contact with what he calls "sense-objects." Many rules are formulated precisely in order to control the reception of stimuli from the sense objects. But lest we get too far ahead of ourselves, we must now return to the text and the next challenge/observation of the *brahmin*.

The *brahmin*'s next challenge is virtually the same as the one we have just examined except the *brahmin* charges that the Buddha is without enjoyment. The Buddha's response is that he does not enjoy forms, sounds, etc. and that enjoyment of the senses has "been cut off at the root like the palm-tree."[3] Again, this refers to the mental control that the Buddha exercises over the stimuli that penetrate through the "doors" of the six sense organs. It is through such mental control that the Buddha then controls his actions in the face of stimuli.

1. *Book of Gradual Sayings* 2 : 16 (brackets in text).
2. Tachibana, *Ethics*, p. 105.
3. *Book of Discipline* 1 : 3.

That leads us to the next observation of the *brahmin* that the Buddha "professes the doctrine of non-action" to which the Buddha replies that he teaches the "non-doing of offences of body, speech, and mind."[1] If we can consider that the sense organs are the "doors" by which stimuli pass through to the mind, then we can also consider that body, speech, and thought represent "doors" or agents of action through which expression passes. In other words, an act is expressed, enacted, or conducted through the agencies of these three modes. Thus, evil actions and good actions are both expressed under these aegis. But the quality of these acts is determined by the disposition or volition of the mind.[2] And that is precisely what the next observation of the *brahmin* is concerned with.

He asserts that the Buddha "professes the doctrine of annihilation." In his response, the Buddha argues that he speaks of the annihilation of passion (*rāga*), hatred (*dosa*), and confusion (*moha*). For the Buddha, these are the "manifold evil and wrong" states of the mind[3] that must be eliminated. Except for the very last exchange, the rest of the Buddha's responses to the *brahmin* are concerned with detesting offences that emanate from the wrong states, restraining those wrong states, and practicing austerities to eliminate the offences of body, speech, and thought and the "evil and wrong states" that give rise to them. We have now come to the crux of the matter of discipline and what it means to act in a disciplined manner.

1. *Book of Discipline* 1 : 4. Cf. *Book of Gradual Sayings* 2 : 200-201 and *Book of Middle Length Sayings* 2 : 222-228.

2. In the *Book of Middle Length Sayings*, idem., we find the following Buddhaic instruction :

"And which, carpenter, are the unskilled moral habits ? Unskilled deed of body, unskilled deed of speech, evil mode of livelihood—these, carpenter, are called unskilled moral habits. Their origination is spoken of too. It should be answered that the origination is in the mind. For the mind is manifold, diverse, various. That mind, which has attachment, aversion, confusion (rāga, dosa, moha), originating from this are unskilled moral habits. These are eliminated by skilled intentions all of which leads to the highest attainments."

3. *Book of Discipline* 1:4. In the *Book of Kindred Sayings*, the Buddha tells a Yakkha that these "wrongful states of mind" come from excessive regard for the self. *Book of Kindred Sayings* 1 : 265-266. Cf. *Book of Gradual Sayings* 1 : 117-119.

First, let us describe how an act transpires according to this initial *Suttavibhaṅga* story : an individual receives stimuli from objects of the senses through his sense organs. If the act is to be of a negative nature, the volition of the mind will be influenced by the "manifold evil and wrongful states" of passion (*rāga*), hatred (*dosa*), and confusion (*moha*). Consequently, the act will be expressed through the agencies of body, speech, and thought. Conversely, disciplined behavior or disciplined acts are motivated by the absence of passion, hatred, and confusion, though still expressed through body, speech and thought. That leads us to the conclusion that the key element in the performance of an act is the condition of the mind. If the mind is influenced by passion, hatred, or confusion in response to external stimuli, an undisciplined act will necessarily follow. This Buddhist formulation represents a refined and sophisticatedly reformulated understanding of the notion of *kamma*. *Kamma* is normally understood to mean "act." However, within the *Suttavibhaṅga* and other early Buddhist texts, it assumes a much more technical meaning : volition or motivation. Indeed, within the *Aṅguttara Nikāya*, we find the often quoted statement attributed to the Buddha :

> O monks, it is volition (cetanā) that I call karma. Having willed, one acts through body, speech, and thought.[1]

That statement requires a bit more attention if we are to realize its full impact.

When *kamma* is understood as volition within the early Buddhist texts, the extreme importance of internal control of the mind is acutely underscored. It is the internal control of volition that enables the *bhikkhu* to act in a detached manner. If the will is controlled, the actions which are directed from the mind will also be controlled. That understanding of volition and act does not, in any way, represent a departure from the more general understanding of *kamma* as a process of cause and effect. Moreover, it represents a more specific application of it. Indeed, the notion that volition conditions the expression of an act is completely consistent with the principle of cause and effect. Just as the results of one act give rise to conditions of another, so the consequence of one's state of mind give rise to the manifest

1. *Book of Gradual Sayings* 3 : 295. Cetanāhaṃ bhikkhave kammaṃ vadāmi; cetayitvā kammaṃ karoti kāyena vācāya manasā.

expression of that state of mind, (or will) through the agencies of body, speech, and thought.[1] Therefore, in a very important sense, the condition of one's mind, whether or not that condition is influenced through ignorance by passion, hatred, or confusion, directly determines the quality of an ensuing act. That is to say, an undisciplined act is the consequence of an ignorant, undisciplined, mind unable to dispel passion, hatred, and confusion. Acts performed with these motivations lead to attachment and further delusion in the chain of causation. On the other hand, a disciplined act is the consequence of an aware, disciplined mind in which the motivations of passion, hatred, and confusion are under control. Acts performed without these motivations prevent attachment and enable the *bhikkhu* to maintain a proper perception of the nature of reality.

In addition to the factor of volition, there are two other elements that are taken into account in the Buddhist analysis of an act : the specific manner in which the act is expressed and the consequences that ensue from an action. At this point in our current discussion, we would like to address the latter issue which pertains to the consequences which ensue from an action.

Varma has pointed out in his discussion of *kamma* that when an action is expressed, "the resultant chain of consequences can be further analyzed at two levels : consequences accruing to the doer or the participant and environmental consequences.[2] Actually, we need not separate the "doer" from his environment. According to the Buddhist understanding of entities, entities cannot exist independently from relations to other entities. An entity or a "being" exists within a perpetual flux of influences. By nature, everything is impermanent and changes from each moment to the next as conditions constantly change. In addition to evaluating intent, the inward quality of a being can be determined by examining its relations to its environment. Being

1. *Book of Kindred Sayings* 2 : 5. Avijjāya kho sati sankāra. hoti, avijjāpaccaya sankhāra. That is, there is a causal relationship between ignorance (avijjā) and volitional activity such that "whenever there is ignorance, there is a tendency for volitional acts to come into being as the result of ignorance." With ignorance dispelled, there is a cessation of volitional activities.

2. V. P. Varma, "The Origins and Sociology of the Early Buddhist Philosophy of Moral Determinism," *Philosophy East and West* 13 (April, 1963) : 27.

is not substantive, but relational and processive. This is exactly what the Buddha meant when he declared that all is impermanence.

The Buddha also taught that as long as a sentient being attempts to search for permanence in quest for satisfaction, he will suffer ceaseless frustration. For, not only do entities exist in a state of relational impermanence, but human beings as entities are also subject to this same fundamental condition. That is to say, there is no such thing as a permanent "self." The notion of an individual substantive "self" is but an illusion. The entire process of seeking gratification is based upon the illusion that a "self" can *possess* other entities.

When this understanding of the nature of entities or "being" is applied to the theory of action which we have been considering, the environmental significance of actions becomes very clear. The significance and consequence of an action must be determined by considering how the action expresses a relation between the doer and his environment. Let us consider the example of the act of killing and its manifold implications for the doer and his environment. The doer will suffer the moral consequences of his action; if the doer is a *bhikkhu,* his community's reputation will suffer; the victim of the action has been deprived of opportunities to advance himself spiritually; and of course, grief will attend to the victim's family.

The doer has reflected the fact that he is not in control of his volition, or, his volition has been influenced by passion and hatred. By its very character, the *bhikkhu* disciplinary code attempts to prevent these types of volitional eruptions by severely restricting the types of occasions that are proper for *bhikkhu* presence.[1] And should a *bhikkhu* be unable to avoid a potentially harmful situation, he is directed to conduct himself inconspicuously, to be completely detached. In other words, the disciplinary code acts as a preventive force by attempting to control the environment of a *bhikkhu* as well as the nature of his actions in relation to the environment.

But once an act such as killing has been transacted, the disciplinary code continues to control the consequences of the act.

1. Kalupahana notes that the Buddha "pointed out that 'living in an appropriate surrounding' (*paṭirūpadesāvasa*) was a factor that contributed to the moral and spiritual advancement of the individual." *Causality*, p. 135.

This is accomplished by the disciplinary precepts which proclaim that such an errant *bhikkhu* be disassociated from the collective *bhikkhusaṅgha.* A *bhikkhu* who intentionally kills another human being is "one who is defeated" and is expelled from the community. The *bhikkhusaṅgha* understands the act of killing as external evidence that the internal condition of the mind is woefully undisciplined. Since a member of the *bhikkhusaṅgha* by definition is supposed to control his inward state, the transgressor, obviously, can no longer be considered as a member of the community. By expelling the errant *bhikkhu*, the *bhikkhusaṅgha* disassociates itself from the condemned action. It thus protects its collective reputation of disciplined purity.

By protecting its collective reputation, the *bhikkhusaṅgha* preserves the status of its own "collective volition." In the chapters to follow on ritual, this concern will be reflected in the great number of qualifications that an applicant must meet before he receives *upasaṃpadā* ordination. This concern is also expressed within the context of the other *bhikkhusaṅgha* rites that we will examine. The aim of Buddhist discipline is directed not only at the spiritual life of the individual *bhikkhu*, but also at the generation and maintenance of purity for the entire *bhikkhu* community. We might say that the sum total of all *bhikkhu* actions reflects the inward condition of the *Saṅgha* as a collective entity. And, we must not forget the nature of an entity : that its quality is determined by its relation to its environment. Members of the *bhikkhusaṅgha* are directly responsible for the status of their community since they form its constituent elements. Their attached or detached, disciplined or undisciplined actions are direct reflections upon the spiritual state of community.

So, the disciplinary code not only seeks to inspire *bhikkhus* to control volition, but also seeks to sustain the collective identity of the community by controlling, to a limited extent, the environmental consequences which follow. By expelling *bhikkhus* for committing actions such as killing, the *bhikkhusaṅgha* purifies its own environment, much in the same way as a king maintains societal order. Discipline, therefore, seeks to regulate the condition of the mind preceding an action and the consequences which follow if that mind persists in an undisciplined manner.

This discussion points to the very intention or basic motivation of the disciplinary code : control through self-effort. An individual *bhikkhu* is responsible for the condition of his mind which is determined by his own abilities to control his volition. The early texts understand volition as *kamma.* Thus, a *bhikkhu* is enjoined to control *kamma.* On another level, the collective community attempts to control the consequences of *kammic* acts through judgments rendered on the basis of the disciplinary code. By expelling *bhikkhus* convicted of errant irregularities, the collective community disassociates itself from the *kammic* consequences that follow. It separates itself from the source of those consequences : the errant *bhikkhu.* By implementing such a separation, it thus maintains a collective identity of an unspoiled nature. For, its "being" is no longer understood, in part, in relation to the errant *bhikkhu* and his evil actions. Hence, the *bhikkhu* disciplinary code represents an attempt to control the process of *kamma* on the level of the individual and on the level of community. Control of that process is directly related to the issue raised in the very last challenge/observation offered by the *brahmin* in the *Suttavibhaṅga* story to which we must now return.

In his last challenge to the Buddha, the *brahmin* says that "The revered Gotama is not destined to another becoming." In response, the Buddha says

> Indeed, brahmin, he whose future conception in a womb, whose future becomings are destroyed and cut off like a palm-tree at the root, are so utterly done away with that they can come to no future existence—him I call one not destined to another becoming. The Tathāgata's future conception in a womb, his rebirth in a new becoming, are destroyed and cut off at the root like a palm-tree, are so utterly destroyed that he can come to no future existence.[1]

In his response to the *brahmin*, Gotama has made it abundantly clear that he will not endure another rebirth. However, his response does not contain a specific rationale for this claim. We must assume, therefore, that this last response represents a conclusion to the discussions that precede it. The Buddha has been engaged in a description of how one can exert self-control of *kamma* (volition). As a result, we must assume that cessation of rebirth is the consequence of controlling *kamma.*

1. *Book of Discipline* 1 : 6.

Our conclusion is warranted for other reasons, however. We can appeal to other early Buddhist texts for support. In the *Mahāsaccaka Sutta* of the *Majjhima Nikāya*,[1] we find a passage that distinguishes two types of actions : *sāsrava* acts that are said to bring about good or bad consequences; and *anāsrava* acts that are based on the knowledge of the Four Noble Truths which lead to *arahan*ship and do not generate good or evil consequences. Similarly, the *Aṅguttara Nikāya*[2] delineates between two types of actions : those performed under the influence of passion (*rāga*), hatred (*dosa*), and confusion (*moha*) which produce bondage; and those actions performed without the influence of the three which lead to deliverance. Finally, according to the *Aṭṭhasālinī* (Buddhaghoṣa's commentary on the *Dhammasaṅgaṇi*),[3] there are four types of acts : (1) evil acts which produce impurity; (2) good acts which produce purity; (3) partly good and partly evil actions producing a combination of purity and impurity; and (4) acts which are neither good or evil and produce neither purity or impurity. La Vallée Poussin interpreted these texts to mean that there are three basic consequences that are derived from actions : good (*kusala*), evil (*akusala*), and neutral (*avyākṛta*).[4] In any case, the Buddha's dissertation to the *brahmin* and passages from these other Buddhist texts make it apparent that motives propelled by passion, hatred, and confusion lead to actions which bear *kammic* fruits. However, it does not follow that actions which are *not* spurred by these three influences must necessarily result in positive fruits. To the contrary, the absence of these three influences indicates that the mind is free from attachment or motive and consequently, no *kammic* results follow. Tachibana has also taken note of this understanding :

> When Buddhahood or Arhatship is reached, actions will bring no effects, because the actions of the Buddha or Arhan are of an inoperative nature, unlike those of the ordinary people. Their actions. . .are not transformed into Kammas, which in the case of the ordinary man, will produce good results in happy or miserable rebirth.[5]

1. *Book of Middle Length Sayings* 1 : 249.
2. *Book of Gradual Sayings* 3 : 128.
3. Buddhaghoṣa *Aṭṭhasālinī*, eds. P. V. Bapat and R. E. Badekar (Poona : Bhandarkar Oriental Research Institute, 1942), p. 73.
4. *Encyclopedia of Religion and Ethics*, 1914 ed., s.v. "Karma."
5. Tachibana, *Ethics*, p. 55.

We have now encountered a crucial notion in our attempt to account for the conceptual basis of discipline. By means of self-control with regard to the sense-organs and the three roots of evil action, the causal law of *kammic* determination can be transcended. With the transcendence of *kammic* determination, the *bhikkhu* is freed from realizing the future fruits of his actions. For, he has performed his actions with volition (*kamma*) under control; he has no vested interest in his actions; he is detached, controlled, disciplined; the cycle of *kammic* rebirth has been shattered. However, his lay counterpart must continue to realize the fruits of actions. Unlike the ideal *bhikkhu* who has eliminated volitional activities, the layman attempts to replace the three evil roots of action with their opposites in an attempt to reap the positive consequences. Yet, because he performs these acts of a positive nature with this knowledge in mind, he remains attached to the motives of action and thus remains subject to *sāṃsāric* existence and *kammic* determination.

Before we attempt to formulate these findings in a manner that will allow us to understand the last three stories which directly preface *pārājika* I (and subsequently the entire *bhikkhu* code of discipline), we must again return to our story at hand for its conclusion.

Following the last exchange with the *brahmin* (which was concerned with the fact that the cycle of rebirth can be broken), the Buddha embarks upon a long monologue in order to explain to the *brahmin* how he came to his knowledge. He reviews how he meditated through the "four musings" in order to attain "purity of mindfulness;" how, during the first watch of the night, he remembered his countless rebirths; how, during the second watch of the night, he discovered the knowledge of the arising and passing away of beings according to their actions; and how, during the third watch of the night, he directed his mind toward the "destruction of the cankers."[1] That knowledge with regard to the "destruction of the cankers" is then made explicit by the Buddha to the *brahmin* :

> I knew as it really is : This is ill, this is the arising of ill, this is the stopping of ill, this is the course leading to the stopping of ill. I knew as it really is : These are the cankers, this is the

1. *Book of Discipline* 1 : 7-10.

arising of the cankers, this is the stopping of the cankers. In me, thus knowing, thus seeing, my mind was freed from the canker of sensual pleasures, my mind was freed from the canker of becoming, my mind was freed from the canker of false views, my mind was freed from the canker of ignorance. (To me) freed, came knowledge through the freedom : I knew : Destroyed is rebirth, lived is the Brahma-life, done is what was to be done, there is no beyond for this state of things.[1]

The Buddha's discourse represents his description of what the convert who has attained the *Dhamma*-Eye will behold. By discovering the Four Noble Truths during the watches of the night, the Buddha gained enlightenment into the nature of reality. The realization of reality, according to the Buddha, is dependent upon the destruction of the cankers. Those who wish that attainment must follow the same path as the Buddha. Armed with the knowledge of the Four Noble Truths, the convert must sojourn along the path of purity in discipline that will lead to unconditioned existence. The *brahmin*, upon hearing the Buddha's testimony, asks for ordination in the fraternity of *bhikkhus*.

Earlier, we mentioned that the *brahmin* was unable to penetrate the teachings of the Buddha because of his ignorance (*avijjā*). By the end of the story, the Buddha has dispelled the *brahmin*'s ignorance. In the *brahmin*'s own words, "In many a figure has the good Gotama made dhamma clear." The *brahmin* is now a converted follower of the Buddha and seeks to implement the teachings of the Buddha in the light of his knowledge of the Four Noble Truths.

In his exchanges with the *brahmin*, the Buddha has explained how one can realize the experience of deliverance. We believe that the way to deliverance, as it has been outlined by the Buddha, reflects an implementation of the Four Noble Truths. People suffer because they are attached to entities that constantly are subject to change in a sea of flux. They perceive these impermanent entities through sense-organs that are not under control. They seek to enjoy these entities motivated by passion, hatred, and confusion. They express these motivations through bodily, verbal, and mental actions which give rise to *kammic* consequences. The *bhikkhu*, on the other hand, realizes that entities are of an

1. *Book of Discipline* 1 : 10.

impermanent nature, that he must control his sense-organs through discipline, that enjoyment of these entities must be resisted, that he must eliminate passion, hatred, and confusion so as not to perform acts through body, speech, and mind which will give rise to *kammic* fruits and hence rebirth. The *bhikkhu*, in short, *believes* in the veritable efficacy of the Four Noble Truths and *acts* through discipline to gain deliverance. Discipline, therefore, is constitutive of the direct path to deliverance and release from suffering.

Now, *nibbāna* is mentioned only twice in the whole of *Vinaya* literature. This should not be such a surprise as the Buddha often refused to speculate about its nature.[1] Many times *nibbāna* is described negatively, bringing to mind the well-known *neti neti* passages of the early *upaniṣads*. Passages from the *Aṅguttara* and *Saṃyutta Nikāya* reveal that *nibbāna* was not understood so much as a space or place in the cosmos, but rather as a mental achievement attained by the perfected *arahan* :

> O bhikkhus, what is the Absolute ? It is,
> O bhikkhus, the extinction of desire [*rāga*],
> the extinction of hatred [*dosa*], the extinction of illusion [*moha*].[2]

Moreover, Horner contends that *nibbāna* "was first a negative term which stood for the waning of wrong states of mind."[3] Only later did *nibbāna* come to mean the waning of the fires of existence. Thus, one who has become *aware* of the nature of existence by attaining the *Dhamma*-Eye, and who thereby comes to monitor his actions through disciplining his volition, has reached the goal. Although this conclusion may seem unsatisfactory to those concerned with the metaphysics of early Buddhism, it is entirely commensurate with an understanding of discipline derived from *Suttavibhaṅga* literature and other early texts. It roots the achievement of such a goal in this very world. Rather than being an "other-worldly" goal, it is an attainment realizable in this-worldly experience. That is to say, *nibbāna* is a state where there is *norm*al happening that is not perverted by a mind-set conditioned by such factors as passion, hatred, and delusion

1. See also *Dialogues of the Buddha* 1 : 300-307.
2. *Book of Kindred Sayings* 4 : 359 and *Book of Gradual Sayings* 4 : 251. See also *Book of Kindred Sayings* 4 : 177 where the Buddha describes *nibbāna* as the absence of passion (*rāga*), hatred (*dosa*) and delusion (*moha*).
3. Horner, *Early Buddhist Theory*, p. 46.

that cause suffering. It is, thus, the *norm*al mode of being gained through the extinguishing of the manifold evil and wrongful states. Disciplined behavior, therefore, should be understood as the product of one who has successfully disciplined his will. A detached or disciplined will gives rise to detached actions that bear no *kamm*ic consequences. The behavior advocated by the disciplinary code represents precisely this kind of discipline. When this discipline is perfected, it is the effective expression of an enlightened will. This may still cause actions, yet the actions are soteriologically fortuitous because they do not generate *kamm*ic consequences.

On the other hand, observance of the disciplinary rules can also be seen as conducive to achieving *nibbāna* or the elimination of an ego-oriented mindset. That is not to say that merely following the letter of the rule causally determines an unblemished will. Rather, it is to say that observing the rules requires mindfulness which in turn leads to a disciplined disposition of detachment. Moreover, by concentrating on performing the right action in a given context, one acts on the basis of what is required in that context to sustain detachment. The prescribed action is held to be proper for the occasion. What this means is that the *bhikkhu* is required to think in terms of detachment, or to think objectively about the context in question, rather than to act spuriously on the basis of unchecked volition. In this way, we can say that discipline is both the cause of detachment and also the consequence of the same. Or better, detached volition arises from awareness of oneself in relation to mental states (passion, hatred, etc.) and in relation to one's total physical environment (*paṭiccasamuppāda*). In both cases, discipline implies not being controlled or determined by either mental forces or by the willy-nilly forces of impermanent flux. It means resisting the current and removing those forces from the mind that result in being swept away endlessly by the stream.

Other early canonical sources point to the crucial importance of observing the rules as a means to attaining the goal. In seven successive "chapters" of the *Aṅguttara Nikāya,*[1] the disciplinary rules are discussed in relation to the path of the *arahan*. In answer to a *bhikkhu* from the Vajjian clan who finds it difficult to recite

1. *Book of Gradual Sayings* 1: 210-216.

and observe the disciplinary rules, the Buddha says that for those who are proficient in *sīla*, *paññā* and *samādhi*, the wrongful states of *rāga*, *dosa* and *moha* will be overcome and no more wicked deeds will be committed.[1] This response would seem to indicate that training in discipline is equated with the *bhikkhu* path in its entirety. And this indication receives full justification in a subsequent passage where the Buddha proclaims the importance of reciting the disciplinary precepts :

> Monks, this recital to be made twice a month amounts to more than one hundred fifty rules wherein are trained clansmen who are eager for their welfare. Now all these combine together to make these three forms of training. What three ? The higher morality, the higher thought, and the higher insight. Herein are combined one and all of these rules.[2]

The next passage refers to one who keeps the rules as one who is also given to mental concentration and insight.[3] And finally, we find a discussion in which the *bhikkhu* who destroys *rāga*, *dosa* and *moha* (and in so doing perfects himself in relation to discipline) is said to "know thoroughly the heart's release, the release by insight, and attaining it abides therein."[4] Such a *bhikkhu* may be reborn once, but he is assured of having made an end of *dukkha*.[5]

Discipline, therefore, is understood in this context to be constitutive of the *bhikkhu* path leading to *nibbāna*. Although other sources indicate that upon perfecting discipline, the *bhikkhu* will continue onward to mount the four *jhāṇic* states of meditation and therein achieve six super knowledges, discipline, by means of mindfulness, is the absolute prerequisite for such an attainment. By destroying or by controlling the "wrongful states of mind" by means of a disciplined disposition, the soteriological destiny of a *bhikkhu* is assured.

Thus, rather than being merely a legal code enforced by sovereign authority or rather than being only an elaboration of *sīla*, the disciplinary code represents the effective behavioral expression which became normative for the path leading to the final spiritual

1. *Book of Gradual Sayings* 1 : 210.
2. *Ibid.*, p. 211.
3. *Ibid.*
4. *Ibid.*, p. 212.
5. *Ibid.*

goal of the religion. The basis of discipline is therefore to be found in the fact that it represents an ideal realization of the teachings of *Dhamma*. In later chapters we shall have further opportunity to see how discipline and *Dhamma* were equated within the ritual context.

But before we address those ritual expressions of discipline, we must first apply our considerations to an analysis of the disciplinary rules as they are presented within the *Suttavibhaṅga*.

Chapter Six

ANALYZING THE DISCIPLINARY RULES

In this chapter, we can apply the results of our discussion in the previous chapter to the *Suttavibhaṅga*'s elaborate presentation of the disciplinary code. Our intention is to classify each of the rules on the basis of a careful reading of the *Suttavibhaṅga* stories that lead up to the proclamation of each rule. That is, we want to pay close attention to the embroidering stories or case histories of each rule. In these stories, we find out why it was necessary for the particular rule in question to be instituted. Thus, our initial schema is aimed at determining which of the three "wrongful states of mind" produced behavior that was considered reprehensible. Secondarily, we shall also classify each action according to the mode of its expression. This means that each action depicted in the stories will be categorized in two ways : the first classification pertains to the kind of motive or attached mindset that produced unacceptable behavior while the second pertains to how that disposition was expressed behaviorally. Thus, the *rāga, dosa, moha*[1] formula will be employed for the former and the body, speech and thought formula for the latter.

We have already noted the great importance attached to controlling the "wrongful states of mind" (*rāga, dosa* and *moha)* in our discussion of the first story of the *Suttavibhaṅga.* These mental forces are understood as the factors that give rise to undisciplined actions. The *Aṅguttara Nikāya* amplifies :

> Monks, there are three causes of the origins of actions. What three ?
>
> Lust, malice and delusion are the causes of the origins of actions

1. It should be clear by now that within the *Suttavibhaṅga* source, the *āsavas* or cankers are equated with *rāga, dosa* and *moha.* This represents a distinct difference from the manner in which the *āsavas* are understood in other contexts. Usually they number five, being often referred to as the "five hindrances." In other sources, *rāga, dosa* and *moha* are identified with the three less attending fetters. But in any case, the function of the two sets remains the same : they serve as the hindrances to achieving a detached disposition.

> Any action done in lust, born in lust, caused by lust, originated by lust is not profitable; it is blameworthy, it has sorrow for its result, it conduces to the arising of further action, not to the ceasing of action.[1]

The absence of these three causes is said to generate actions not conducive to further arising.[2] And finally, ego-oriented desire is identified as the source of these three "wrongful states of mind."[3] Quite simply, we are arguing that the stories leading up to the proclamation of each rule implicitly describe actions generated out of wrong intent or motivation. And, that these motives, or "wrongful states of mind," are rooted in excessive concern for the self. Each rule, therefore, represents a device invented by the Buddha or the *Saṅgha* to prevent the expression of such a motive. When the rule is observed, or when one is mindful of the reason for the rule, the *bhikkhu* ideally acts in the absence of these motives. Or better, the *bhikkhu* acts "purely." That is, he will act in a manner *detached* or *apart* from wrongful intent.

This *purity* of intention is said to give rise to perfected expressions of purity. Again, the *Aṅguttara Nikāya* defines the nature of this purity :

> Monks, there are these three forms of purity. What three? Purity of body, purity of speech, and purity of thought.[4]

The meaning of purity in these expressive forms of behavior is then described at length.[5] Purity of body is described in terms of abstaining from taking life, from stealing and from sexual misconduct. Purity of speech is described as refraining from lying and idle babble. Purity of thought is described as not being malevolent or covetous and having a right view. It should be evident that the types of behavior described in this *Aṅguttara Nikāya* passage correspond to the major concerns of the *pārājikas* and consequently to the entire disciplinary code. Our task is to coordinate the motives of undisciplined actions with their behavioral expression as indicated in the literature. When

1. *Book of Gradual Sayings* 1 : 241. The same stock phrase occurs in connection with malice (*dosa*) and delusion (*moha*) in immediately following passages.
2. Ibid., p. 243.
3. Ibid., pp. 243-244.
4. Ibid., p. 249.
5. Ibid., pp. 249-251.

the *Suttavibhaṅga* literature is viewed in this light, it reveals a syllogistic pattern : selfish desire allows one's volition to be influenced by *rāga, dosa* and *moha* which in turn generate actions expressed through body, speech, or thought requiring *kamm*ic retribution. Disciplined behavior, on the other hand, involves acting *apart* (*Vinaya*) from desire for the self, and thus in the absence of *rāga, dosa* and *moha.* Behavior that is expressed through body, speech and mind therefore is not conducive to further becoming because of its intrinsic purity. In short, detached volition gives rise to detached actions which result in detachment from becoming. Pure expressions of body, speech and thought are reflections of a pure disposition.

We can now begin our analysis by turning to the three stories that serve as prefaces to the first *pārājika.* We will then proceed to an analysis of the rest of the disciplinary rules.

In the first story, a certain Sudinna, the son of a wealthy merchant meets the Buddha, listens to the *Dhamma*, and asks the Buddha for ordination into the fraternity of *bhikkhus.* The Buddha admits him with the condition that Sudinna obtain parental consent. After considerable pleading by his parents, they finally give him their reluctant consent. Meanwhile, Sudinna's mother conspires with Sudinna's wife : the plan is for Sudinna's wife to seduce Sudinna so that she may bring forth an offspring to inherit the family's wealth The next day, Sudinna makes his alms rounds and comes to the house of his parents where his parents again plead with him to live "the low life of a layman, both to enjoy riches and to do meritorious actions." Again Sudinna spurns their pleas. Later when the conspiracy is hatched, Sudinna's mother goes to where Sudinna lives in the Great Wood and explains to him that his family's wealth will be lost to the Licchavis if he does not produce an heir. Finally, Sudinna consents and impregnates his wife who bears him a son. Sudinna becomes physically sickened and confesses his sin to the *bhikkhus.* In rote fashion, he is rebuked and the matter is reported to the Buddha who then admonishes Sudinna and expells him from the order.[1]

There are several matters in this richly illustrated story which could warrant detailed consideration. For example, the

1. *Book of Discipline* 1 : 21-38.

characterization of the lay life as "low," a prospective *bhikkhu*'s need for parental authorization, and the fact that Sudinna becomes physically ill during the same time that he becomes remorseful about his sexual engagement. Howsoever interesting these details may be, we must save them for a later study and direct our concerns toward Sudinna's motive and his method of expression. Sudinna's motive for sexual intercourse with his wife is activated by his mother's plea for an heir to inherit the family's riches. Though Sudinna resists the plea to a certain extent, he finally consents because he still retains an abiding value in the wealth of his family's possessions and the continuation of his family's material heritage. He has failed to constrain his passion and attachment to the value of riches even though he engages in sex for the gain of his family and not for himself. He is thus guilty of *rāga*, though his passion is not necessarily of the sexual brand. Because he engages in sexual intercourse to achieve his end, his motive is translated into action through the means of bodily expression. Sudinna is therefore expelled from the community because of his incapacity to control *rāga*. When it becomes public that his wife has been impregnated by him, it becomes evident that he has expressed *rāga* through the bodily mode. His expulsion from the fraternity of *bhikkhus* maintains the collective purity of the group by disassociation. The community remains untainted by Sudinna's inability to restrain *rāga*.

The second story involves a short tale that we have already encountered[1] about how a certain bhikkhu "on account of his lust kept a female monkey." As we recall, when the *bhikkhu* was on his alms round in the village one day, a company of *bhikkhus* happened upon his *vihāra*. They were greeted by the monkey who "postured before them." They concluded that the *bhikkhu* of this *vihāra* had engaged in sexual intercourse with the monkey and asked the *bhikkhu* about the matter when he returned. He admitted to the accusation but defended himself by saying that the injunction against sexual intercourse "refers to the human woman and not to the female animal." He was rebuked by the *bhikkhus*, the matter was reported to the Buddha, the *bhikkhu* was summoned, confessed, and expelled from the order by the Buddha.[2]

1. See pp. 56-57.
2. *Book of Discipline* 1 : 38-40.

Again, there are facets of this story which could occupy our attention. For instance, the element of living alone apart from the cenobitical community, etc. But the important issue at stake in this story remains the *bhikkhu*'s attempt to circumvent the disciplinary code. His defence for engaging in sexual intercourse with the monkey is inadmissible. The nature of the offence is not changed by simply substituting the object of passion. For, *rāga* still remains the compelling motive and the act is still bodily expressed and consummated.

The third story is a bit more complex and, according to Horner, it may not be of the highest antiquity.[1] The story concerns a group of *bhikkhus* who lived ostentatiously by drinking, eating, and bathing as they desired. They lived their lives by "not having paid attention to the training, but not having disavowed it." As part of their life-style, they frequently engaged in sexual intercourse. They all fell on hard times and confronted Ananda to ask him if they might receive another ordination "in the presence of the lord." Ananda tells the Buddha about these *bhikkhus* and the Buddha refuses their request on the basis that they were well *aware* of the training rules when they committed their sexual acts. Therefore, they are ineligible for the *upasaṃpadā* ordination.[2] Ino ther words, they cannot become full members of the *bhikkhu* community, nor are they to be in communion with the community as each "is one who is defeated."

As usual, there are very interesting materials in this story as in the others. For instance, the *bhikkhus* who carry on living the life without restraints eventually fall upon hard times. That eventuality signifies the moral retribution that is involved in the process of *kammic* determination. But, the fundamental issue of this story revolves around the request of the indigent and penitent *bhikkhus* to receive full ordination despite the fact that they committed their transgression with full knowledge of the disciplinary code. The fact that they are refused and pronounced "not in communion" and "defeated" again underscores the determination of the order to maintain its collective identity. For, these *bhikkhus* were considered as members of the fraternity "having gone forth under this dhamma and discipline which

1. Horner, *Book of Discipline* 1 : 41, note 1.
2. *Book of Discipline* 1 : 40-42.

are well taught." Because they were cognizant of the prohibition against sexual intercourse, they cannot be considered confused, ignorant, or bewildered as to the rule's intent and meaning. Therefore, their guilt, which springs from their attachment to a certain life-style and passion for sexual activities, cannot be forgiven. They have expressed their guilt through their admission of engaging in sexual intercourse. Had they disavowed their training and made no pretense about conforming to the disciplinary code, they would have been able to receive *upasaṃpadā*. But, since they attempted to keep their Buddhist *bhikkhu* identity while engaging in a reprehensible life-style, they are subject to dismissal from the order on the basis of *pārājika* I.

It should be evident that these stories are rich materials that provide us with illustrative portrayals of early *bhikkhu* life. Through our method of classification, we cannot claim to exhaust the meaning of each of these stories in the *Suttavibhaṅga*. We can only point to the conceptual structure behind the formulation of these tales. We should also point out that the brief tales, which in many cases *follow* the definition of the rule at hand, also provide very significant insights into the degree of culpability of particular *bhikkhus* in various circumstances. For instance, there are many of these brief tales that indicate that a *bhikkhu* is not guilty of a *pārājika* offence (expelled from the community) if he engages in sexual intercourse without knowing it. Strange as that may sound, there are a number of brief tales[1] in which a monk is sleeping and a woman sits upon his penis. When the *bhikkhu* confesses this happening to the Buddha, he is found not guilty if he did not consent to the action. The point here is that with the absence of motivation or intent, a *bhikkhu* cannot be held responsible for engaging in acts that he does not self-motivate.

Within the *Suttavibhaṅga,* there is an inordinate amount of trust put into the accounts of culpable or innocent *bhikkhus* who are under question. Further, *bhikkhus* also seem extraordinarily willing to confess their transgressions to the Buddha and usually do so in the exact same wording used by the *bhikkhus* who have reported the matter back to the Buddha. This seems to indicate a paradox : whereas a *bhikkhu* may be so undisciplined that he

1. *Book of Discipline* 1 : 59-63.

commits an act such as killing or sexual intercourse, he always willingly confesses his act to the Buddha. Why should a *bhikkhu* capable of committing the worst sins not also be capable of lying about his transgression ? By confessing his evil, he has forfeited any chance of remaining in good standing with the fraternity of *bhikkhus.* There are at least three possible answers to render this paradox understandable.

In the first case, these stories do not attempt to provide a comprehensive depiction of a *bhikkhu*'s personal nature, but rather consist of single-minded descriptions of acts which were judged by the Buddha to be unacceptable; i.e., the *bhikkhu* is not the subject of the story, but the nature of the transgression is the topic. Secondly, there is no advantage to lying to the Buddha. For, the opening lines of the *Suttavibhaṅga* describe him as "all-knowing." Thirdly, a *bhikkhu* has already been excommunicated in reality from the collective community by virtue of his misconduct. Therefore, he is now subject to *sāṃsāric* existence and the law of *kammic* retribution. Further misconduct can only worsen his future condition.

It is within the context of these stories that we shall seek to discern the motives and modes of expression that comprise acts of an undisciplined nature. Each story provides us with examples of behavior deemed unacceptable to the early *bhikkhu* community. Whether or not they are grounded in historical fact is not the issue here. We are interested, however, in the fact that these stories convey the communal understanding of what does and what does not constitute discipline. Therefore, we shall now turn to the *bhikkhu* disciplinary code in its entirety and present our findings in terms of our classification schema. We shall consider each classification of the rules as they are presented in the text beginning with the *pārājikas*, then the *saṅghādisesa*, the *aniyatas*, etc.[1] In each case, we shall present our findings for each class of offences and then provide a brief discussion.

Table 2

MOTIVATIONS AND EXPRESSIONS OF THE *PĀRĀJIKAS*

Motivation		*Means of Expression*	
rāga—	1a 1b 1c 2a 2b 3b 4a 4b	body—	1a 1b 1c 2b 3a
dosa—	3b 4b	speech—	2a 3b 4a 4b
moha—	2a 2b 3a 4b	thought—	3b 4b

1. The numerical designations correspond to the number that is assigned

One of the first things that we immediately notice is that a motivation or an expression can be of mixed fashion. For example, in the second story which prefaces *pārājika* 4, which we have labelled as 4b, a group of *bhikkhus* lied about their spiritual status because "the heart...yielded to passion, their heart yielded to hatred, their heart yielded to confusion."[1] Correspondingly, the mode of expression in this same story takes the form of both speech and thought. The minds of the six *bhikkhus* were deluded into *thinking* that they had attained what they had not attained. As if that expression were not enough, they proceeded to boast verbally about their unfounded claim.

With regard to *pārājika* 2, the injunction against stealing or taking what is not given, it seems only natural that the motive for this act be that of greed and attachment. As our chart indicates, that holds true to form to a degree. However, theft or taking what is not given also arises due to ignorance or confusion about what can be properly appropriated. In 2b, a group of *bhikkhus* assume that it is admissible to take "a bundle of things that have been bleached" if the bundle is found in the jungle and not in the village.[2] In *pārājika* 3, we would suspect that the motive for killing might always be found in hatred. Yet that is not the case. In 3a, *bhikkhus* have heard a discourse from the Buddha about purity of the body and are vexed by their own physical impurities. Thus, they employ a "sham recluse" to kill them so they will be rid of their bodies.[3] Hatred of the body might be understood as a motive for this form of suicide. But confusion or ignorance about the intent of the Buddha's teaching is the identified motive in the story as the Buddha proceeds to clarifyhis position.

Table 3

MOTIVATIONS AND EXPRESSIONS OF THE *SAṄGHĀDISESAS*

Motivation		*Means of Expression*	
rāga—	1a 2a 3a 4a 5a 5b 6b	body—	1a 2a 7 13
dosa—	4a 8 9 10 13	speech—	3a 4a 5a 5b 6 8 9 10 11 12 13
moha—	7 11 12 13	thought—	8 9 10

to the rule in question within the *Suttavibhaṅga*. When two or more stories preface the declaration of a rule, we have labelled the first story as "1a," the second as "1b," etc.

1. *Book of Discipline* 1 : 158.
2. Ibid., p. 172.
3. Ibid., pp. 116-123.

The *saṅghādisesa* rules are grouped together because they consist of disciplinary rules that, when broken, require a formal meeting of the order. If a *bhikkhu* is convicted of one of these offences, he is temporarily suspended from the order and must undergo the *mānatta* discipline. This form of discipline is designed to correct the *bhikkhu*'s tendency to think that his "self" is an independent and permanent entity. Thus, it would seem that a *bhikkhu*'s condition of ignorance (*avijjā*) or confusion (*moha*) would be responsible for his breakdown in this disciplined conduct. There can be no doubt that *avijjā* is related to every motivation that propels undisciplined behavior.

However, our stories also indicate more specific mental conditions that lead to disciplinary irregularities which are the product of ignorance. In fact, we have a rather even distribution of "wrongful" mental influences in the *saṅghādisesas*. The first five rules are concerned with a *bhikkhu*'s conduct toward women. Then, two injunctions follow which address the building of huts and *vihāras* and attempt to prevent *bhikkhus* from overbegging building materials from the laity and from building where harm might befall living creatures. The last six rules involve violations expressed through speech to create schism, to defame, or to purposely quarrel. The first nine rules contain brief stories following the rule's declaration, but the last four do not. Evidently, the editors or compilers of the text believed that the stories which precede each respective declaration sufficiently made clear the application of those rules of training. In any case, we find some interesting peculiarities in these rules. For instance, story 1b, which we encounter in chapter four,[1] is of a very different nature and we have been unable to classify it along with the others. It concerns the unintentional emission of semen during a dream. The Buddha declares that there is no offence for such an occurrence. Although such an occurrence might indicate that a *bhikkhu*'s mind is not completely subdued, such an act has not been intentionally performed and is therefore excusable. In that connection, we can also point out the often occurring disclaimer that a *bhikkhu* is not guilty of an offence if the offender is "mad, unhinged, in pain, or a beginner." Again, we have confronted the principle that an act is dependent upon

1. See pp. 53-55.

conscious volition and becomes an undisciplined act if a *bhikkhu*, with the knowledge of the course of training, purposively performs a transgression. But without that factor of conscious volition (with the knowledge of the course of training), a transgression is excused.

Finally, with reference to the *saṅghādisesa* rules and to all other rules as well, an expression may some time take two forms. Motivated by hatred, a *bhikkhu* might not only defame another, but attempt to inflict bodily injury. Or motivated by hatred, a *bhikkhu* may formulate a plan (thought) that is executed through verbal means. That is precisely the case in *saṅghādisesas* 8, 9, and 10. Therefore, at times we must classify acts within two or three categories of expression.

Table 4

MOTIVATIONS AND EXPRESSIONS OF THE *ANIYATAS*

Motivation		*Means of Expression*	
rāga—	1 2	body—	1
dosa—		speech—	2
moha—		thought—	

The two *aniyata* rules are classified together because they are matters which are "undetermined." The two stories involve brief narratives about the lascivious Udāyin who seeks to sit with a young woman in a "secluded and convenient place." Thus, that which is undetermined is that which the lecherous Udāyin might try to do under those circumstances. *Aniyata* 1 hints that sexual intercourse might be the possible act and *aniyata* 2 hints that it might be lewd words. In any case, an investigation has to be supported by "lay women" who will provide evidence to determine the transgression and thus the suitable punishment. In both cases, the obvious motivation for getting a young woman into a "secluded and convenient place" is passion.

Table 5

MOTIVATIONS AND EXPRESSIONS OF THE *NISSAGGIYAS*

Motivation							*Means of Expression*						
rāga—	1a	1b	2a	2b	3	4	body—	1a	1b	2a	2b	3	4
	5a	6a	6b	7	8	9		5b	6a	6b	7	16	19
	10	11	12	13	14	16		24	25	29			
	17	18	19	20	21	22							
	23	24	26	27	28	30							
dosa—	15	25					speech—	5a	6a	8	9	10	11
								13	14	17	18	20	21
								22	25	26	27		
moha—	29						thought—	4	15	23	28	29	30

By the time we reach this section of the *Suttavibhaṅga*, we are definitely dealing with minor offences. Even the brief narratives following the rule's declaration have been largely dropped. However, a short paragraph still remains to discuss various applications of the rule and to pronounce "no offence" for monks who are "mad," "beginners," etc. These brief paragraphs still reflect the importance of determining the intent of the *bhikkhu* in question. But they are very terse and straight to the point. Here is an example of these scholastic formulations which follow the declaration of the rule :

> If he thinks it is bartering when it is bartering, there is an offence of expiation involving forfeiture. If he is in doubt as to whether it is bartering, there is an offence involving forfeiture. If he thinks that it is not bartering when it is bartering, there is an offence of expiation involving forfeiture. If he thinks that it is bartering when it is not bartering, there is an offence of wrong-doing (dukkata). If he is in doubt as to whether it is not bartering, there is an offence of wrong-doing. If he thinks that it is not bartering when it is not bartering, there is no offence.[1]

This example of scholastic formulations again reflects the importance of the *bhikkhu*'s intent. Each change in the circumstances with regard to what the *bhikkhu* thinks, and what he does, slightly changes the offence that is determined. That type of detailed attention is typical of the excruciatingly fine precision given to the application and understanding of a rule's meaning.

As Table 5 indicates, almost all the *nissaggiyas* can be accounted for through *rāga*. Attachment results in wrongful possession of articles and fantastic attempts to hold on to them. Sixteen rules are concerned with robes, five with rugs, three with gold and silver, two with bowls, one with medicine, and one with wrongfully taking benefits intended for the entire order. Roughly a half of the rules are designed to prevent *bhikkhus* from asking for too much from their supporters. The rest are designed to teach *bhikkhus* to use what they have properly and not to use more than is absolutely essential. Six times we run into double formulations of the rules. The second formulation is one that receives the characteristic carefully worded definition. That

1. *Book of Discipline* 2 : 111-112.

reflects the fact that some rules had to be amended because they were of an impractical nature. Thus, in *nissaggiya* 6, we find the prohibition of receiving robes from anyone who is not a relation. But a second story relates how a *bhikkhu* had been robbed of his robe and in order not to wander about naked, received a robe from an unrelated householder. That event is related to concern for maintaining a distinct identity. Much of the minute attention to robes, bowls, etc., indicates great concern for maintaining a proper appearance that not only distinguished the *bhikkhu* from the householder, but in the case of the *bhikkhu* who would have had to go on without a robe, distinguished the Buddhist from the Jaina. Finally, we must also note that the *nissaggiyas* are rules which are definitely preventive in nature and not retributive. These injunctions are aimed at encouraging the *bhikkhu* to use goods in a proper manner. Attachment only leads to more craving and a more difficult path to the perfectly disciplined state.

Table 6

MOTIVATIONS AND EXPRESSIONS OF THE *PĀCITTIYAS*

Motivations							*Means of Expression*						
rāga—	7b	8	10	11	16	21a	body—	5	6	10	11	16	18
	21b	25	30	31	32	34		20	25	27	28	29	30
	35	37	38	39	43	44		31	32	33	34	35	37
	45	47	51	57	59	62		38	40	41	43	44	45
	86	87	88	89	90	91		48	49	50	51	52	53
	92							54	55	56	57	58	59
dosa—	1	2	3	4	7c	9		60	61	62	66	67	69
	12	13	17	20	21	24		70	74	75	78	80	83
	36	32	48	49	50	54		85	87	88	89	90	91
	55	60	61	63	65	66		92					
	70	74	75	76	77	78							
	79	82	85				speech—	1	2	3	4	7a	7b
moha—	5	6	7a	10	11	14		7c	8	9	12	13	16
	15	18	19	22	23	26		17	21a	21b	22	23	24
	27	28	29	33	40	41		31	32	33	34	35	36
	46	52	53	56	58	64		39	42	46	47	54	55
	67	68	69	71	72	73		60	63	64	65	67	68
	79	80	81	83	84	85		69	70	71	72	73	76
	87	88	89	90	91	92		77	79	81	82	85	86
								87					
							thought—	14	15	19	61	78	80

With the *pācittiyas*, we encounter rules formulated on a myriad of subjects. Most of the rules are of an extremely minor nature and many of the stories are so brief that it becomes very difficult to determine an explicit motive for the wrong-doing under consideration. In such cases, we have attempted to warrant our choices with careful reflection. Many of the offences were the direct result of a *bhikkhu* not being aware of the implications of his act that had been performed with absolutely no evil or wrongful intent.

For example, in *pācittiya* 6, the *bhikkhu* Anuruddha is invited by a woman to spend the night with her in her house because the guest-house is full. She, being a lovely thing to look at, attempts to seduce Anuruddha by taking her clothes off and begging him to enjoy her. But Anuruddha, described by the text as one who is completely restrained with regard to his senses, does not so much as look at her and refuses her invitation. Then, he preaches *Dhamma* to her and she decides that she wants to become a lay devotee of the Buddha. Further, she admits her shame. When the Buddha hears this story, he pronounces an injunction against sleeping with women under any circumstances.[1] *Pācittiya* 7 and 84 also contain prefacing stories where no stretch of imagination can ascertain an intentional motive for a wrongful act.[2] In these and other stories, we have had to classify the motive in terms of ignorance, or *moha*. Evidently, the point of these stories is to emphasize the potentially dangerous context that a *bhikkhu* has allowed himself to fall in to. Again, this reflects the preventive nature of the disciplinary code.

Some of the stories that we encounter in the *pācittiyas* are virtually the same ones that we have found in prefaces to *nissaggiya* declarations. In addition, a number of *pācittiyas* are no more than formal recastings of the same material found in earlier rules, particularly *pārājikas* 3 and 4. That evidence would indicate that the *pācittiyas*, in general, may represent later formulations inspired by discussions of rules that had already been formulated.

We also find a great deal of modification included within this group of rules, presumably in the spirit of moderation. Many

1. *Book of Discipline* 2 : 198-201.

2. *Pācittiya* 7 is found at *Book of Discipline* 2 : 203-204 while *Pācittiya* 84 is found at *Book of Discipline* 3 : 77-78.

rules are prefaced by stories that have been obviously expanded and, with each expansion, a new and qualified expansion of the declaration follows. Sometimes, a story is followed by another brief story in which the Buddha begins a reformulation with the phrase "I allow." These devices no doubt reflect corrections to basic rules that were felt to be reasonable and not contrary to the essential purpose of discipline. One can almost visualize a "middle way" of moderation being forged within the context of these individual rules.

Finally, we must again emphasize that the purpose of these rules is first and foremost the lesson of discipline. Collectively, these rules manifest an incredible degree of concern for appearing and acting in a specified accord that is not only conducive to the spiritual quests of the *bhikkhus*, but also meets with the approval of the laity, the chief supporters of the *bhikkhu* community. In almost every case with the *pācittiyas*, a rule is formulated because the laity had grumbled about the actions or appearance of the "Sakya Sons."

Table 7

MOTIVATIONS AND EXPRESSIONS OF THE *PĀTIDESANIYAS*

Motivation							*Means of Expression*						
rāga—							body—	1		3a	3b	3c	4
dosa—							speech—		2				
moha—	1	2	3a	3b	3c	4	thought—	1		3a	3b	3c	4

The four rules that comprise the sixth section are known as the *pātidesaniyas* and are all concerned with the proper procuring of alms. Violation of any of these four rules needs only to be confessed. The overriding concern of these rules is to make sure that obtaining alms in no way causes hardship for the giver. The first, third and fourth *pātidesaniyas* contain stories to illustrate this point. In the first, a *bhikkhu* accepts alms from a generous *bhikkhuni* on four successive days. As a result of giving her own food away, she has become so famished that she is unable to go out to procure alms for herself. In the third story, *bhikkhus* are told not to accept alms from families who have become "learners." This designation is rare, for it represents an agreement between a faithful family of adepts and the *Saṅgha* which relieves the family of their obligations to provide alms for the *bhikkhus*. The reason given for this agreement is the fact that such a family decreases in wealth and cannot afford to contribute without causing hardship. The fourth rule is concerned with making sure that laity who set out to give alms to *bhikkhus* living in the jungle are forewarned if there are thieves in the area. In each of these cases, we observe an overriding concern that others do not suffer on account of giving to *bhikkhus*. That is, *bhikkhus* ought not to be a source of hardship. As a field of merit, *bhikkhus* who are on alms rounds represent opportunities for laity to perform acts that increase personal merit. However, *bhikkhus* must be aware of the circumstances in which they receive alms. If it is to the physical detriment of the giver, or if it is beyond reasonable means, the *bhikkhu* must take care to insure that such giving is not detrimental. Although we might understand the taking of alms in these circumstances to be the result of greed or attachment on the part of the *bhikkhu*, the breaking of these precepts is more likely the result of not paying attention to the situation at hand, or being dull-witted. We have thus categorized these stories as the result of *moha*. Correspondingly, the act is both a negligence of thought as well as body.

The second *pātidesaniya* acquaints us with the apparent *bhikkhuni* counterpart to the *chabbaggiyas*. These mischievous six nuns are found to be busy giving orders to the laity as to where, when and to whom alms should be given. But the rule in question does not directly concern their ostentatious behavior. Rather, the rule is directed toward *bhikkhus* who would permit such behavior. *Bhikkhus* who do not restrain *bhikkhunis* in these circumstances are guilty of violating the rule. Again, failure to do so seems to be the consequence of the dull-witted to address the *bhikkhunis* in question.

In sum, the *pātidesaniyas* reflect *bhikkhu* concern for making sure that the laity are not in some way alienated or caused suffering through the practice of almsgiving. Observance of these rules can be assured by one in whom concern for others takes precedence over concern for self.

Sekhiyas

The *sekhiyas* number seventy-five in total and constitute formulations that are, at first glance, of an even more minor nature than those of the *pācittiyas*. As such, the specific intentional motivation cannot be perfectly gleaned from the prefacing stories. Indeed, many, if not most of the declarations, are stated positively beginning with the phrase "I shall." Implicit in these declarations is the understanding that since a *bhikkhu* is disciplined, he will express himself perfectly in the way referred to in the rule's declaration.

Lest our readers believe that we have admitted that our classification system is not sufficient to accommodate these rules, we offer this consideration : more than any other classification of disciplinary rules listed in the *Suttavibhaṅga*, the *sekhiya* rules demonstrate that discipline of one's inward state is of the utmost importance to the spiritual life of the *bhikkhu*. That statement might sound paradoxical in the light of the fact that most scholars have described the *sekhiyas* as matters of social etiquette and politeness. But, these rules are much more than mere social etiquette : they are outward reflections of the inner state of a *bhikkhu*'s mental condition. The fact that they are so concerned with matters that appear to be of such a minute nature is evidence that a disciplined mental culture was expected to be manifested in even the most meticulous fashion.[1]

Superficially, we can agree with Horner that the rules can be arranged into three segments : (1) rules 1-56 which focus upon appearance and etiquette during alms rounds; (2) rules 57-72 which pertain to making sure that *Dhamma* is taught and heard with respectful propriety; and (3) rules 73-75 which are concerned with unsuitable ways of urinating and spitting.[2]

However, we must also point out that one's outward appearance was symbolic in at least two ways. In the first case, *bhikkhus* were considered to be "sons of the Buddha" and objects of veneration for the laity. To appear in public in a dishevelled fashion was insulting not only to the Buddha, but to the laity who considered *bhikkhus* as examples of high Buddhist spirituality and worthy receptors of meritorious acts of lay piety. In the second

1. This great importance attached to outward appearance is noted by Horner in *Early Buddhist Theory*, pp. 94-95, where she comments on the conversion story of Sariputta. Sariputta has just encountered Assajji and is very impressed by his orderly and serene appearance. In describing Sariputta's response, Horner writes : "For here it (*arahan*) is used of a man whose demeanor makes Sariputta curious to know who was his teacher. He detected the man's inner worth through his outward appearance."

2. Horner, Introduction to the *Book of Discipline* 3: xxviii.

case, *bhikkhus* were bearers of the *Dhamma* and the chief source of learning for the laity. Casual attention to one's public habits would reflect a similar casual regard for the teaching of the *Dhamma*. By this, we mean to argue that the *sekhiyas* are more fundamentally concerned with expression. The motive which generated their inclusion into the disciplinary code was quite simply this : perfect control of inward demeanor leads to perfect control and awareness of outward expression, even the most minute public expressions. Furthermore, it provides us with a reason for the fact that many of the *sekhiyas* are declared in a positive fashion unlike the prohibitory declarations that characterize the first six *Suttavibhaṅga* classifications. Thus, we find for *sekhiya* 1 : "I will dress with the inner robe all round me."[1]

Therefore, with respect to the *sekhiyas*, it is not so important for us to determine the motive behind each declaration in the manner we have for the other sections of rules. One motive governs all declarations : comprehensive discipline untainted in every detail. We therefore offer only a classification of expression : body—1-56 and 73-5; speech—57-72. All of these rules require the conscious attention of the *bhikkhu*. As such, a *bhikkhu* must constantly focus his thoughts upon his disciplined appearance. In other words, his bodily and verbal expressions must be coordinated by thoughtful readiness that is the result of his disciplined mental culture. A thoughtful expression is required by every *sekhiya* determination.

Adhikaraṇasamatha

This last classification within the *Suttavibhaṅga* does not really contain *Pāṭimokkha* disciplinary rules *per se*. It consists of seven ways to settle disputes. No stories preface these declarations, no definitions or elaborations are provided; they are simply listed. In the spirit of the *Vinaya*'s barebones treatment of these seven "rules," we shall simply quote their entry in the text :

> These seven rules, venerable ones, for the deciding of legal questions come up for recitation : for the deciding, for the settlement of legal questions arising from time to time a

1. *Book of Discipline* 3 : 121.

verdict in the presence of[1] may be given, a verdict of innocence may be given, a verdict past of insanity may be given, it may be carried out on (his) acknowledgment, (there is) the decision of the majority, the decision of specific depravity, the covering up (as) with grass.

In this chapter, we have argued that *bhikkhu* discipline can be best understood as the self-control of one's inner condition. Self-control of one's inner condition, however, cannot be effected without the essential knowledge of the Four Noble Truths which accurately depict the process of dynamic becoming. But once that knowledge is received and accepted, it is possible to embark upon the path of discipline which leads to deliverance. Deliverance entails the cessation of suffering through the breaking of the cycle of rebirth. We have argued at length that, according to the *Suttavibhaṅga* and the *Nikāyas*, the cycle of rebirth can only be broken through control of *kammic* consequences. In that connection, we have demonstrated the manner in which *bhikkhu* utilization of the disciplinary code represents an attempt to control *kammic* consequences on the level of the "doer" and on the level of environment (of which the community is a part). *Kammic* consequences can only be controlled through the destruction of the three cankers : *rāga*, *dosa*, and *moha*. It is when these three cankers, together with the undisciplined acceptance of stimuli through the sense-organs, are allowed to influence the condition of the mind that undisciplined acts expressed through bodily, verbal, and mental modes occur. By proper discipline, a *bhikkhu* is able to eliminate motivations which give rise to acts that entail *kammic* consequences. Thus, if there is an essential lesson to be learned from the *Suttavibhaṅga* literature, it is that undisciplined behavior, which is generated out of selfish desire, leads to a continuation of suffering. On the other hand, for the *bhikkhu* who has become aware, who attains to a disciplined disposition, actions performed in the absence of ego-oriented motives lead to the realization of the goal : selflessness.

In this chapter, we also noted the collective concerns of the *bhikkhusaṅgha* to maintain a status of collective purity. With the death of the Buddha, his followers assumed the primary

1. The presence of the Order, of *Dhamma*, of Discipline and of persons disputing. *Book of Discipline* 3: 153-154.

responsibility for maintaining and furthering the teachings of the master. As such, the *Saṅgha* assumed a position of great authority within the Buddhist community as a whole. The *Saṅgha* came to be understood as the preservers of *Dhamma*, the teachers of *Dhamma*. Since its collective identity rested upon the reputations of its individual members, it could not afford to be lax in discipline. Failure to maintain order would result in a loss of status. Thus, its "corporate state of charisma" was a matter of vital interest. In the following two chapters, we shall see how portions of the *Mahāvagga* concerned with ritual expression address this need for maintenance of collective purity.

CHAPTER SEVEN

RITUAL EXPRESSIONS OF *BHIKKHU* DISCIPLINE : *UPASAMPADĀ*

Whereas *Suttavibhaṅga* literature is primarily addressed to the disciplined behavior of the individual *bhikkhu*, the *Khandhakas* section of the *Vinaya* is essentially concerned with the collective acts of the community. As we stated in our introduction, the *Vinaya* has bifocal concerns : the spiritual quest of the individual through discipline and the collective spiritual experience of the community. What ties these two concerns together is discipline. In the next two chapters, we shall examine ritual expressions of the *Vinaya* that constitute a cultic celebration of discipline.

The *Khandhakas* section of the *Vinaya* differs considerably from the *Suttavibhaṅga*. Where the *Suttavibhaṅga* is organized around the various classes of disciplinary rules, the *Mahāvagga* and *Cullavagga* contain diverse materials[1] loosely strung together amid a biographical account of the Buddha's missionary career. The origins of the *Saṅgha* and the instituting of the primary collective rituals are established by the Buddha for the purpose of furthering *Dhamma*. Like the *Suttavibhaṅga* formulations, whenever an instruction is given by the Buddha, endless variations follow. The *Cullavagga* especially insists upon untiringly explicating the exact and proper conditions for settling disputes, for administering probation (the *mānatta* discipline), for holding

1. There is absolutely no doubt that much of the *Khandhakas* materials that make up the stories that preface a proclamation of the Buddha are borrowed from other sources and embellished to suit the occasion. It is possible to locate the original source in a number of these cases; for example, the story of Soṇa Kolivisa in *Mahāvagga* V, 1 is also found in *Aṅguttara Nikāya* III, 374-379 (*Book of Gradual Sayings* 3: 266-70). However, some stories that are obviously borrowed from other sources cannot be located in other sources available to us. For instance, the long story about how Jīvaka Komārabhacca became a renown doctor (which is inserted as a preface to the Buddha's proclamation that it is allowable to wear householder's robes) is certainly a legend that has been appropriated for use in the *Khandhaka*, yet we find it nowhere else in the Pāli canon. See *Mahāvagga* VIII, 1; *Book of Discipline* 4 : 379-97.

the *Pāṭimokkha* recitation, and for the proper adjudication of the *Saṅgha*'s "formal acts." Again, we meet with materials that are the product of scholastic love for exactitude and precision.

The *Mahāvagga* and *Cullavagga* are comprised of distinct chapters (*khandhakas*) in which the origins of significant communal institutions are related in these formal, precise terms. But, the chapters are more than mere handbooks or compendia. They reflect a consistent concern for the proper expression and execution of *Dhamma*. This concern is evident throughout the chapters up to and including accounts given of the First and Second Great Buddhist Councils. These last accounts serve as concluding appendices and demonstrate how the enduring *bhikkhu* community manifested its concern for the maintenance of discipline. This is especially the case with the account of the Second Great Buddhist Council, and it is only fitting that the *Vinaya* concludes on that note.[1]

Although the *Vinaya*'s accounts of the first two Buddhist councils have often been the subject of study, the *Vinaya*'s depiction of ritual has been ignored for the most part. Within the general field of history of religions, and particularly among those scholars who study Asian religions, ritual has been often treated as the silent cousin of myth. Without question, the results of many stimulating essays on the religious significance of myth in Asian traditions have been prodigiously satisfying to students who are interested in understanding the Asian religious imagination. Yet too often the ritual dimension of religious expression, the arena in which religious man's creative ideas are frequently translated into formal deeds, are eclipsed by the scholar who centers his attention solely upon cosmology, soteriology or dogma. Over a generation ago, Paul Levy decried this general state of affairs within the realm of Buddhist studies :

> The fact that Buddhist ceremonial has not given rise to a large amount of theorising does not make it any less important; what is left of it (for it is rapidly disappearing) bears witness to the part it formerly played. That this was an important one is confirmed by the content of ancient texts.[2]

1. Here, we do not include the *Pārivara* which consists of a long appendix of matters mostly addressed previously within the *Vinaya*.

2. Paul Levy, *Buddhism : A Mystery Religion* ? (New York : Schocken Books, 1968), p. 3. Although Levy's book deals very perceptively with the

In these following pages, we shall examine the *Vinaya*'s treatment of *upasaṃpadā*, the ordination procedure prescribed for those wishing to gain full status within the Buddhist *bhikkhusaṅgha*. In so doing, we shall explicate how the early *bhikkhusaṅgha* defined its own nature as a collective whole and how considerations to preserve that identity led to strict requirements and prerequisites for an individual who desired to become one of its members.

Before we focus our exclusive attention upon that task, some remarks about the nature of ritual are imperative. Ritual can be analyzed from a variety of perspectives. Two of the more compelling approaches can be generated from the interpretations of rites of passage articulated by Arnold van Gennep and Mircea Eliade. In his classic work *Les rites de passage*, van Gennep stressed the *transitional* function of ritual that accompanies passage from one given status to another :

> For a man to pass from group to group—for example, for a peasant to become an urban worker, or even for a mason's helper to rise to mason—he must fulfil certain conditions, all of which have one thing in common : their basis is pure economic or intellectual. On the other hand, for a layman to enter the priesthood or for a priest to be unfrocked calls for ceremonies, acts of a special kind, derived from a particular feeling and a particular frame of mind. So great is the incompatibility between profane and sacred worlds that a man cannot pass from one to the other without going through an intermediate stage.[1]

The intermediate stage that van Gennep refers to is none other than the rite of passage, a formal act that facilitates the passage from one recognized passage or identity to another. As such, rites of passage not only lead to a new identity for the ritual participant, but they also reveal the means by which a community defines itself. That is to say, an individual seeking ordination into a religious community must conform to that community's standards of measurement which define membership. By becoming a member of the community, the individual participates in and sustains the identity of the community.

significance of *upasaṃpadā*, we will not share his approach. Fundamentally, Levy argued that the *upasaṃpadā* represents a dramatic recollection of the events of the alleged First Great Buddhist Council.

1. Arnold van Gennep, *The Rites of Passage* trans. by M. Vizedom and G. Caffee (Chicago : The University of Chicago Press, 1960), p. 3.

From another perspective that is by no means exclusive of van Gennep's position, Eliade emphasizes the *regenerative* aspect of initiation rites. Eliade contends that initiation rites signal a paradigmatic expression of "the end of a mode of being—the mode of ignorance" and of irresponsibility.[1] Hence, the goal of initiation procedures is the creation of a new man who has been reborn into a new spiritual life. Ignorance is dispelled as the important teachings of the community become known to the initiant. Thus for Eliade, initiation procedures reflect the process by which a new man is *made.*

> It is the old initiates, the spiritual master, who make him. But these masters apply what was revealed to them at the beginning of Time by the Supernatural Beings; indeed, in many cases they incarnate them. This is as much to say that in order to become a man, it is necessary to resemble a mythical model.[2]

The initiant becomes a member of the community when he assumes the collective heritage that is grounded in the paradigmatic prototype of a mythical model. With regard to monastic Buddhism, this means that the neophyte who has joined the *bhikkhusaṅgha* assumes the identity forged by the Buddha as perceived from within the *bhikkhu* tradition.

The very first chapter of the *Mahāvagga* portion of the Pāli *Vinayapiṭaka* is entitled *Mahākhandhaka* or "Great Section."[3] Although this initial chapter represents the longest single entry within the entire *Vinayapiṭaka,* there are a good many other reasons for the title it bears : it contains an account of the Buddha's experience of enlightenment and the formulation of his Four Noble Truths, his decision to preach *Dhamma* publicly and his initial missionary converts, his performance of miraculous wonders,[4] and the conversion of two of his chief disciples

1. Mircea Eliade, *Rites and Symbols of Initiation* (New York : Harper and Row, 1958), p. xiii.
2. Ibid., p. xiv.
3. *Book of Discipline* 4 : 1-129.
4. *Book of Discipline* 4 : 28-29, 30-31, and 32-45. Within these units of the *Mahākhandhaka,* the Buddha's control of magic is introduced. In *Mahāvagga* I, 11 and 13, the Buddha conquers the power of Māra (death) by elimination of the lure for pleasures of the senses and by the destruction of the fetters of existence. In units 15-20, the Buddha demonstrates his magical powers and his omniscience. Clearly, the implication of these passages is that the Buddha, by virtue of his discovery of *Dhamma,* has gained complete *control* over all the powers of existence.

(Sâriputta and Moggallâna).[1] After the narrative has described those events within the first twenty-four units of the *Mahākhandhaka*, the main subject of the chapter becomes evident: admission to the fraternity of *bhikkhus*. But this preface has served an extremely important function : the spiritual charisma of the Buddha is established and his first converts are won. The portrait of the Buddha in this preface is especially significant, for he becomes the mythical model to be emulated by future generations of *bhikkhus*. As we have seen, he is seen as the omniscient Tathāgata who enforces the rules of discipline to facilitate the spiritual quests of his disciples. But also, the Buddha cuts the figure of one who embodies *Dhamma* and *Discipline*.

In any event, the relationship between the preface to the *Mahākhandhaka* and its main subject, *upasampadā*, is really quite clear. Rhys Davids and Oldenberg are very explicit on this point :

> The regulations regarding admission to the fraternity, which are discussed in this Khandhaka, could not but present themselves to the redactors of the Piṭaka as being the very basis of their religious discipline. It was possible to fancy the existence of the Saṃgha without Pāṭimokkha rules, or without the regulations about the Pavāraṇā festival, but it was impossible to realise the idea of Saṃgha without rules showing who was to be regarded as a duly admitted member of the fraternity and who was not. It is quite natural, therefore, that the stories or legends concerning ordination of the bhikkhus were put in connection with the record of the very first events of the history of the Samgha.[2]

The comment by Rhys Davids and Oldenberg is incisive on several counts. In the first case, by associating *upasampadā* with the first events of the *Saṅgha*, legitimacy is conferred upon its character because it has been instituted by the authoritative figure of the Buddha. Secondly, this association allowed the redactors of the *Vinaya* to present an ideal image of the earliest community which was later to become a standard. And finally, the characterization of the earliest *Saṅgha* as a community that shares in the Buddha's vision of the truth (*Dhamma*) is a powerful apology. In essence, the redactors presented a conception of the *Saṅgha*'s

1. *Book of Discipline* 4 : 55-57.
2. Rhys Davids and Oldenberg, *Vinaya Texts* 1 : 73, note 1.

collective identity as being intricately related to the *Dhamma* of the Buddha.

It is in regard to this last point that the contributions of Max Weber about the importance of charisma become especially relevant for our discussion. Weber distinguished between two types of charisma : personal charisma and charisma of the office. The former is grounded in the special relationship existing between the sacred and the individual. In the case of the Buddha, charisma derives from the fact that he had realized existentially the truth and power of *Dhamma*, a realization recognized by his followers as valid. Weber was intent upon delineating between two types of individuals who possessed charisma :

> Thus, there remain only two types of prophets in our sense, one represented most clearly by the Buddha, the other with especial clarity by Zoroaster and Mohammad. The prophet may be ... an instrument for the proclamation of a god and his will, be this a concrete demand or an abstract norm. Preaching as one who has received a commission from god, he demands obedience as an ethical duty. This type we shall term the "ethical prophet." On the other hand, the prophet may be an exemplary man who, by personal example, demonstrates to others the way to religious salvation, as in the case of the Buddha. The preaching of this type of prophet says nothing about a divine mission or an ethical duty of obedience, but directs itself to the self-interest of those who crave salvation, recommending to them the same path as he himself traversed. Our designation of this second type of prophecy is "exemplary."[1]

Our findings support this conclusion when the disciplinary rules are understood as constitutive of the path leading to *nibbāna* rather than being ethical demands derived from a deity or sovereign authority on high. We have endeavored to make this very case in previous chapters.

As Weber continues his discussion :

> Regardless of whether a particular religious prophet is predominantly of the ethical or predominantly of the exemplary type, prophetic revelation involves for both the prophet himself

1. Weber, *Sociology of Religion*, p. 55; cf. Wach, *Sociology of Religion*, pp. 37-41.

> and for his followers—and this is the element common to both varieties—*a unified view derived from a consciously integrated and meaningful attitude toward life.*[1]

As we noted in chapter five, all of the Buddha's initial converts shared the vision of the Buddha by means of having attained the *Dhamma*-Eye. All new *bhikkhu* converts were admitted to the *Saṅgha* by virtue of "having penetrated the truth." In short, the *bhikkhu* community shares the charisma of the master by virtue of the fact that they emulate the model he provides through adhering to discipline. And, as we have attempted to demonstrate, discipline is the effective application of the world view articulated by the Buddha in his sermon on the Four Noble Truths. It is in this vein that we must understand the *Mahākhandhaka*'s account of the founding of the *bhikkhusaṅgha* : the collective identity of the community must be understood as grounded in its perfect understanding and application of the Buddha's declared *Dhamma.* In effect, the text has succeeded in describing the community in terms of a "pristine past," a golden age *in illo tempore* when all members shared in the realization of *Dhamma.* When the first *bhikkhus* were converted by the Buddha, their ignorance was dispelled and the beginning of a new spiritual life began. Thus, the ordination of new members was rather simple consisting of the Buddha's inducement :

> Come, O Bhikkhu, well taught is the doctrine; lead a holy life for the sake of the complete extinction of suffering.[2]

With the origins of the *bhikkhu* community depicted in such an ideal light, it was necessary for the redactors of the *Mahāvagga* to describe how the ordination procedure evolved from such a simple inducement to the manner in which *upasaṃpadā* was conducted in their own time. To accomplish this task, we find a second mode of *upasaṃpadā* also being described in the last half of the twenty-four unit preface of the *Mahākhandhaka.* This second type of *upasaṃpadā* procedure serves as an effective textual device to bridge the gap between the original ordination transaction and the complex ritual that we shall soon meet. In this intermediate stage in the text's account of the *upasaṃpadā* evolution, we have the first delegation of "Buddhaic" authority and

1. Weber, *Sociology of Religion*, pp. 58-59 (emphasis mine).
2. *Book of Discipline* 4:19.

the inclusion for the first time of taking refuge in the *triratna* ("the triple gem"—the Buddha, the *Dhamma* and the *Saṅgha*). The account of this second *upasampadā* procedure is given within the context of a *bhikkhu* community that is rapidly expanding and becoming increasingly mobile. The inconvenience of travel and the fatigue that accompanies such travel are the reasons given for granting ordained *bhikkhus* permission to confer *upasampadā* to new converts. Picking up the story in *Mahāvagga* I, 12, 3 :

> I grant you, O Bhikkhus, this permission :
> Confer henceforth in the different regions and in the different countries the pabbajjā and upasampadā ordinations yourselves. And you, O Bhikkhus, ought to confer...in this way : Let him who desires ordination first have his hair and beard cut off; let him put on yellow robes, adjust his upper robe so as to cover one shoulder, salute the feet of the Bhikkhus and sit down squatting; then let him raise his joined hands and tell him to say : "I take refuge in the Buddha, I take refuge in the Dhamma, I take refuge in the Saṃgha. And for the second time...And for the third time..."[1]

Although our narrative has cited explicitly the reasons of distance, travel, growth of the order and inconvenience for the delegation of authority to perform *upasampadā*, a more subtle operation is at work in the text. This second stage in the evolution of the rite must be understood in relation to the first. As the text has made explicitly clear, all members of the *bhikkhusaṅgha* who have been initiated by the Buddha possess the *Dhamma*-Eye. It is only natural, therefore, that these bearers of the Buddha's *Dhamma* be invested with authority to admit new members. That which is being implicitly stated in this development is this : the Buddha's personal presence is not crucial for *upasampadā* to be performed; rather, the presence of the perfect *Dhamma* (whether represented by the Buddha or by one of his disciples) is the *sine qua non* that makes *upasampadā* efficacious. Thus, it is the authority of the Buddha's *Dhamma* which is shared by the *bhikkhusaṅgha* that makes ordination an authentic transaction. The new protagonist of the *Mahākhandhaka* account thereby shifts from the personal fetes of the Buddha to the charisma invested in the *bhikkhusaṅgha*. The fact that the

1. *Book of Discipline* 4 : 30.

original members of the *bhikkhusaṅgha* possess the *Dhamma*-Eye establishes the fundamental relationship between the personal charisma of the Buddha and the charisma of his order. When the personal presence of the Buddha is no longer, i.e., when he passed into his *pārinibbāna*, the presence of his *Dhamma* that was shared with his disciples remains with the continuing *bhikkhusaṅgha*. Therefore, we find in this stage of *upasaṃpadā* development as it is presented within the text a connecting link between the original simple inducement and the final framing of the *upasaṃpadā* with which the rest of the *Mahākhandhaka* is concerned. We are now ready to attend to the many modifications which accompany the fully developed *upasaṃpadā* procedure as depicted in our text. These various qualifications will give us more clues as to the precise means by which early Buddhist adherents measured the eligibility of aspiring converts.

Immediately following the *Mahākhandhaka* preface, the structure of the *bhikkhusaṅgha* assumes more complexity, probably reflecting the actual state of the monastic community at the time the *Vinaya* received its root form. In *Mahāvagga* I, 25, *bhikkhus* go out on alms rounds wrongly dressed, beg[1] for alms, and act in a boisterous manner.[2] As is the usual pattern in *Vinaya* literature, the laity begin to grumble about this unbecoming monastic behavior, their grumblings are overheard by modest *bhikkhus* who report the matter to the Buddha who in turn summons and rebukes the offending *bhikkhus*. After a severe admonition, the Buddha declares that each newly admitted *bhikkhu* be assigned to a preceptor.[3] It is the chief duty of the preceptor to teach his pupil in matters of *Dhamma* and discipline. In return, each pupil is to become the personal attendant of the preceptor.[4] The relationship between the two is characterized in a paternal fashion :

1. "Begging" is not quite the proper word here as *bhikkhus* and laity did not understand making the alms round as begging; rather, the alms round provided the laity with an opportunity to acquire merit by contributing to the welfare of the *bhikkhusaṅgha*.
2. *Book of Discipline* 4: 57-58.
3. An *upajjhāya*.
4. The complete list of duties that each is responsible for keeping is found in *Mahāvagga* I, 25-37, *Book of Discipline* 4: 57-85. A *bhikkhu* may not become an *upajjhāya* unless he has been a full member of the *bhikkhusaṅgha* in good standing for a minimum of ten years. A pupil may be dismissed by

> The upajjhāya, O Bhikkhus, ought to consider the saddivihārika [pupil] as a son; the saddivihārika ought to consider the upajjhāya as a father. Thus these two, united by mutual reverence, confidence, and communion of life, will progress, advance, and reach a high stage in this doctrine and discipline.[1]

That there was such a need to institute a novice status is highly significant. In the first case, the text is betraying the fact that at an early point in the history of the *bhikkhusaṅgha* it became necessary to establish a period of training before an aspiring *bhikkhu* would be granted full status through the *upasampadā* ordination ritual. It is now apparent that all newly admitted *bhikkhus* are no longer considered to have become immediately enlightened, or have attained *Dhamma*-vision, "having penetrated the Truth," etc. In order to preserve the ideal identity of full *bhikkhu* status, a course of training had to be laid out. The *pabbajjā* admittance to the order is the preliminary requisite and a period of time must pass in which the aspiring *bhikkhu* demonstrates his worthiness to receive *upasampadā*. That this *pabbajjā* institution became so regularized and highly defined indicates that we are definitely dealing with a portion of the text depicting the *bhikkhusaṅgha* at a highly developed stage, a stage in which the monastic order can no longer afford the luxury of admitting anyone who seeks ordination even if they claim to perfectly understand *Dhamma*. The *bhikkhusaṅgha* has been forced to become selective in its attempt to maintain its collective identity. A *bhikkhu* who became troublesome presented at least two problems : he distracted attention from the pursuit of the spiritual life and he also caused the prestige of the monastic order to suffer in the eyes of lay supporters.

This textual development adds a twist to the importance of discipline. Whereas the early portions of the text depict all newly ordained *bhikkhus* as converts to the Buddha's world view, i.e., the attainment of *Dhamma*-Eye, this is apparently no longer the case. Consequently, discipline must be considered in a different fashion. In the case of those converted by the Buddha in the early portions of the *Mahākhandhaka*, discipline is the effective

his preceptor if he does not show affection to his teacher, if he has no faith in his teacher, if he is not humble, if he is not respectful, and if he does not exhibit spiritual development (*Mahāvagga* 1, 27, 6; *Book of Discipline* 4 : 70).

1. Ibid., pp. 58-59.

expression of the perspective inherent in *Dhamma*-vision. But in later portions of the text that outline the *pabbajjā* institution for novices, discipline is seen as a means to achieving full *bhikkhu* status, a means by which the individual may demonstrate his worthiness to become a full-fledged member of the monastic order.

But the institution of the teacher/pupil relationship and the period of training therein were not the only qualifications added as the *Mahākhandhaka* exposition continues. As the text moves forward to its climax and the finalized version of the *upasampadā*, we discover numerous stories that further qualify who will be eligible to join the *bhikkhusaṅgha*. All of these qualifications serve to make the order more elite and special. These qualifications are further safeguards against admitting those who would cause internal friction, problems with the laity, and those who do not possess a serious disposition toward the perfection of religious discipline. We shall now review some of these qualifications to see what types of individuals were excluded from membership.

In *Mahāvagga* I, 39, we are told that at one time in the kingdom of Magadha, the people were afflicted by a plague, leprosy, boils, consumption and fits. The local doctor was so busy that he could not possibly tend to all of the sick. Considering the situation, some men put forward the proposition :

> What if we were to embrace the religious life among the Sakyaputtiya Samanas : then the Bhikkhus will nurse us, Jīvaka Komārabhacca will cure us.[1]

These people were given *pabbajjā* and ordination, nursed by the *bhikkhus* and cured by the doctor, Jīvaka Komārabhacca. The *bhikkhus*, so as to be able to continue nursing the many sick newly admitted members, had to solicit excessively from the laity. And because the doctor had been ordered by Bimbisāra, King of Magadha, to care for all sick *bhikkhus*, most of his time was spent caring for the *bhikkhusaṅgha* while his other duties among the laity were neglected. Subsequently, some of the newly admitted and cured *bhikkhus* left the order and "returned to the world." The doctor recognized these people, became angry, and reported the matter to the Buddha who in turn announced a prohibition

1. Ibid., pp. 89-90.

against ordaining anyone afflicted with a disease. The point to this story is that *upasampadā* can only be conferred upon individuals whose motives for joining the monastic order are not connected to attached worldly concern. The *bhikkhusaṅgha* must not be used for ulterior motives. When ulterior motives become the basis for joining the *bhikkhusaṅgha*, it not only causes confusion within the order, but also wreaks havoc upon its lay supporters.

The same principle applies to a number of stories that follow concerning a soldier who joins the monastic community to avoid combat duty,[1] a robber and a prisoner who seek to avoid prosecution,[2] a person heavily in debt attempting to avoid paying his bills,[3] a slave seeking escape,[4] a young man who had quarreled with his father and had run away,[5] youths under twenty years of age who want to live a leisurely existence,[6] and immature boys under fifteen years who might be mistaken for being a biological son of an *upajjhāya*.[7] After a series of nine stories concerning regulations for novices,[8] the litany of exclusions

1. Ibid., pp. 91-92. Rejecting soldiers who wish to join the *bhikkhusaṅgha* may seem paradoxical in the light of the *Vinaya*'s deep-rooted concern for *bhikkhus* not killing any living beings. This concern is most emphasized in the third *pārājika* offence considered at length in the *Suttavibhaṅga.* We might also be tempted to recall Arjuna's moral dilemma in the *Bhagavad Gītā*. However, the argument here is not about caste duty; instead, the principle at work here with regard to rejecting soldiers has to do fundamentally with volition. For a candidate to be admitted to the order, he must not join for reasons of escaping worldly obligations. Rather, candidates must display a genuine concern for taking up the *bhikkhu* path for spiritual reasons.

2. Ibid., pp. 93-94. Not only would a robber avoid prosecution since according to *Mahāvagga* I, 42, 2, King Bimbisāra had granted immunity to the order, but he would also gain a perfect guise for further theft. In these three stories, we again find the laity becoming a critical concern to the *bhikkhus*; for, it is their complaints which lead to the formulation of this specific exclusion.

3. Ibid., p. 95.

4. Ibid., pp. 95-96.

5. Ibid., p. 96.

6. Ibid., pp. 96-98.

7. Ibid., pp. 98-99. In the case related in this story, the young boy is actually the son of a newly ordained *bhikkhu*. But the point of this exclusion is that if *bhikkhus* appear to have offspring, they have broken the primary disciplinary prohibition against engaging in sexual intercourse.

8. These nine stories (Ibid., pp. 52-60) dictate certain regulations that are to be observed by novices (young boys who have received the *pabbajjā*

continues : eunuchs,[1] imitators of *bhikkhu* life-style,[2] animals,[3] those guilty of matricide and patricide,[4] those who have killed *arahats*,[5] those who have committed rape,[6] a hermaphrodite,[7] those who do not have a proper *upajjhāya*,[8] one who does

ordination) : two novices may not have the same preceptor out of fear that they might commit sodomy with each other during the adolescent years (I, 52); *pabbajjā* may not be conferred without parental consent (I, 54); a learned competent *bhikkhu* may ordain more than one novice—a relaxation of I, 52—(I, 55); the ten precepts of training are made explicit and include the *pañcaśila*, eating at forbidden times, abstinence from dancing, singing, or creating music, abstinence from wearing garlands, and abstinence from receiving gold or silver (I, 56; it should be noted here that these are the same precepts that the laity were asked to follow during the *Uposatha* observance); punishment of novices must not include the deprivation of food (I, 57, the point here being that *bhikkhus* should not deprive novices of anything that has been provided for the community by the laity); a novice may not be punished without the consent of his preceptor (I, 58); one *bhikkhu* may not "draw the followers of another *bhikkhu* over to himself" (I, 59); ten cases lead to the expulsion of novices from the community including the breaking of the five *pañcaśila* rules, speaking against the Buddha, the *Dhamma*, and the *Saṅgha*, espousing false doctrines, and engaging in sexual intercourse with a *bhikkhunī* (this last rule being redundant since sexual intercourse is prohibited in the *pañcaśila*) (I, 60). *Mahāvagga* I, 51 is an allowance to admit novices of 15 years old or younger "if they can scare crows" (a relaxation of I, 50—see note above). *Mahāvagga* I, 53 contains the account of how the Buddha's son, Rahula, asked for his inheritance from the Buddha. Rahula receives the Buddha's *Dhamma* as his inheritance. This story is to serve as a paradigm for the teacher-pupil relationship as well as the relationship between the Buddha and his order. Just as a worldly father leaves his material inheritance to his son, so the *Saṅgha* receives its spiritual inheritance from the Buddha and a novice receives spiritual inheritance from his preceptor.

1. Ibid., pp. 108-109.
2. Ibid., pp. 109-110. "Imitators" is a reference to those imposters who assume *bhikkhu* apparel in order to obtain alms from the laity.
3. Ibid., pp. 110-111. The rationale for excluding animals is that animals are beings who are incapable of spiritual growth and must wait for the fruits of former acts to mature before they can be transformed into humans. Only humans can effect changes in status or make spiritual progress. See pages 120-122.
4. Ibid., p. 112.
5. Ibid., pp. 112-113.
6. Ibid., p. 113.
7. Ibid.
8. Ibid., pp. 113-114. The list of those who are ineligible for becoming preceptors is approximately the same list for those who are excluded from the order.

not possess a bowl or robe,[1] and one who is physically deformed.[2]

There is no question that these exclusions were designed to keep the *bhikkhusaṅgha* free from involvement in troublesome cases and to protect its collective image from becoming tarnished. The exclusions appear to be based upon consideration of three factors : a candidate's motivation to join the *bhikkhusaṅgha,* his moral background, and his physical capabilities. With regard to the first two considerations, it is not difficult to imagine why the monastic order felt obliged to reject such candidacies. These exclusions point to the fact that the *bhikkhusaṅgha* would accept only those aspirants who desired ordination on the basis of proper volition. We cannot emphasize this importance of volition enough. As we have seen within the *Suttavibhaṅga* portion of the *Vinaya,* the character of one's volition necessarily determines the quality of one's expression. That is to say, the inward condition of one's being is manifest in one's outwardly observable acts. Although the disciplinary rules enumerated within the disciplinary code of the *Vinaya* seek to regulate these outward behavioral expressions, the principle of discipline applies to all components of an act : beginning with the contact between the object of the senses with the sense organs, to the mind's response to that contact, to finally the verbal, mental or bodily expression that is a consequence of the mind's volition. We have noted that the key to this understanding of action is that volition is understood as *kamma*. *Kamma* is that which must be controlled, disciplined; for, it is the consequence of one's undisciplined volition that results in actions that bear fruit and thereby perpetuate entanglement in the world. Only by disciplining one's volition, one's will, can a *bhikkhu* hope to cut himself off from desires that lead to continued rebirth and attendant suffering. By admitting *bhikkhus* to full ordination for any other reason than a genuinely expressed will to sojourn the path that leads to *nibbāna,* is to invite contradiction and open the *bhikkhusaṅgha* to concerns motivated by a worldly orientations of the attached kind. The consequence of admitting individuals for any other reason than proper volition entails the inevitability of coping with the future undisciplined acts perpetrated by the newly admitted candidate.

1. Ibid., pp. 114-115.
2. Ibid., pp. 115-116.

Although membership in the *bhikkhusaṅgha* may be regarded in one sense as an attempt to escape the snare of worldly entrapments, it was by no means to be considered as a haven for social misfits. Even though the path of the *bhikkhu* is a way to control the consequences of *kammic* retribution, it does not provide blanket pardons to eradicate the fruits of one's former actions. The control of volition must come from the dedicated effort of the individual. It does not simply accrue to newly admitted members or is not considered a gift from the *bhikkhusaṅgha* to its members. Thus, a *bhikkhu*'s charisma is not the type described by Weber as charisma of the office, a quality that can be assumed merely by occupying a specified position within social hierarchies. Rather, the monastic community offers instruction in the path to *nibbāna* in an environment conducive to its attainment. Therefore, to admit candidates with such questionable motivations for joining is contrary to the *bhikkhu* ethic of discipline. Further, it would have the effect of drawing the community into interaction with a number of third parties : kings seeking to punish robbers, killers and military deserters, parents seeking to find runaways, and bill collectors trying to locate debtees, etc. The worldly concerns of these parties, though legitimate, distracts from the formal concerns of the *bhikkhusaṅgha.* In addition, the harboring of such candidates does nothing to sustain the pristine image of the *bhikkhu* heritage or its contemporary relations with the laity. In order to preserve the community's collective identity based upon dedication to attaining release from the endless cycle of rebirth, it was thus necessary to exclude candidates with questionable motives or undisciplined volitions as measured by their behavior.

It is also not so difficult to determine the reason why non-humans and physically deformed individuals were not allowed to receive *upasampadā.* With regard to the former, cosmological considerations prevented non-human membership. Within Buddhist cosmology, there are six realms within conditioned existence : the realm of the gods, the demons, human beings, animals, ghosts, and souls in hell. The distinction between each realm is not permanent, however. Only those humans who have entered the path to *nibbāna* will escape from endlessly passing from one of these forms of existence to another dependent upon the fruits of action. Within this cosmological schema, humans constitute the fundamental agents of action. In order to attain *nibbāna*, one must be born in a human status in one's last rebirth. According to Tambiah,

> Central to the Buddhist doctrine is that to be born as a human being is a privilege because it offers the only opportunity for betterment and final liberation through one's decisive effort.[1]

In other words, the entire cosmos is focused upon man as the determining agent. It is impossible for other types of beings to assert change in status. This cosmological fact is graphically illustrated in the *Petavatthu* ("Stories of the Departed") where hungry ghosts plead with human beings to act on their behalf, i.e., to transfer the merit of human actions in order to forge a change in cosmological status. Only human beings can effect a change in their future cosmological fate or make an effort to transcend conditioned existence. Given this understanding, the *bhikkhusaṅgha* had no choice to reject beings of a non-human status.

With regard to human beings who had been deformed in a certain manner, we can only offer matters of a practical nature as possible explanations. If one was deaf, how could *Dhamma* be heard ? If one could not walk, how could alms rounds be made ? If one's fingers were cut off, how could the alms bowl be held ? etc. The point of this exclusion seems to be the same point made in *Mahāvagga* I, 39. That is, the *bhikkhusaṅgha* cannot act as a nursing home for the infirm. As each individual is responsible for his own spiritual progress, so must he be able to take care of his own physical body. Although this may seem to be a rather callous attitude, it indicates the extreme emphasis placed upon individual responsibility within the *Vinayapiṭaka*. That does not mean that *bhikkhus* would not care for each other in times of illness. It only means that the *bhikkhusaṅgha* was a community committed to the maintenance of conditions conducive to the spiritual fruition of its members. It is quite possible that these last exclusions may date back to very early times when wandering *bhikkhus* spent nine months in temporary residences. Such a life-style would not permit constant care for invalids.

Having presented all of these qualifications, the *Mahākhandhaka* moves into its climax with a detailed description of the *upasampadā*

1. Stanley J. Tambiah, *Buddhism and the Spirit Cults*, p. 40.

rite. Up to this point, the text has made it clear how the original *upasampadā* came into being and which individuals are eligible for ordination. The narrative now sets out to describe how ordination is to be conferred and what necessary prescriptions must be taken immediately following the procedure.

Actually, the description of the *upasampadā* consists of what has been previously proclaimed in the *Mahākhandhaka*.[1] The candidate and his *upajjhāya* appear before an assembly of at least ten fully ordained *bhikkhus*. The *upajjhāya* proclaims that his pupil desires to receive ordination and appoints himself or another learned *bhikkhu* to publicly question the candidate about the "disqualifications." But before the questioning begins, the candidate is told to adjust his robes properly and to raise his hands respectfully as he says three times :

> I ask the Saṅgha, reverend Sirs, for the upasampadā ordination : might the Saṅgha, reverent Sirs, draw me out of compassion towards me.[2]

Then the public questioning about the disqualifications ensues. The candidate is asked about his status as a free man, his masculinity, his financial state, his military status, his family obligations, his age, and whether or not he possesses a robe and bowl, etc. Having answered satisfactorily and having been declared freed of the "disqualifications," the questioning *bhikkhu* asks the assembly on behalf of the candidate to approve the request for ordination. By silence, the request is approved. Then the assembly of *bhikkhus* tell the member what season and date it is so that the new member will always know his correct "spiritual age." Finally, the new member is told about the "four resources"

1. See *Book of Discipline* 4 : 29-30, 71-73, and 80-85. These units respectively include the account of the Buddha giving authority to *bhikkhus* to ordain new members by means of the *triratna*, the account of how a majority vote determined whether or not a candidate would be accepted, and the account of the founding of the preceptor-novice relationship. When the concerns of these three accounts are combined with the "four interdictions" (see page 123), all of the principal elements of the *upasampadā* as it is practiced today have been taken into account. For descriptions of *upasampadā* as it is practiced today, see Levy, *Buddhism*, pp. 4-60.

2. Ibid., p. 122. Here we can allude to the fact that it is now the compassion of the *Saṅgha*, rather than the Buddha, that results in the *bhikkhu* becoming a member.

consisting of alms, robes of rags, dwelling at the foot of a tree,[1] and the use of decomposing urine for medicinal purposes.[2]

At this juncture in the text, *upasampadā* would appear to be complete. However, two more modifications are appended that underscore the importance of discipline for the newly ordained *bhikkhu.* The first modification is presented within the context of a story in which a newly ordained *bhikkhu* is left alone and subsequently encounters his wife. She tells him that since sexual intercourse is difficult to obtain for those who "have gone forth," he should indulge with her. He does, is questioned by *bhikkhus* about his absence, and the matter is reported to the Buddha. In turn, the Buddha prescribes that newly ordained *bhikkhus* must not be left alone until the "four interdictions" have been explained to him. The four interdictions are then recounted and correspond to the first four cardinal precepts *pārājikas* of the disciplinary code elucidated in the *Suttavibhaṅga* portion of the *Vinaya.*[3] This is highly significant because the "four interdictions" represent the types of prohibited behavior that can result in expulsion from the community. The breaking of the *pārājikas* symbolizes that the individual is really unfit to proceed further along his path to *arahan*ship because he lacks the disciplined volition necessary for its perfection.

The second modification is presented within a story about a *bhikkhu* who was guilty of a wrong-doing and refused to admit his guilt, left the order, and later returned asking to be reinstated. The text relates that if he admits his guilt, he is reinstated and must then make amends for the wrong-doing.[4]

The *Vinaya*'s portrayal of the development of the *upasampadā* ordination yields a detailed picture of monastic concern for its own image, an image to be assumed and sustained by each newly admitted member. A newly admitted *bhikkhu,* having satisfactorily cleared himself of the many disqualifications enumerated within the textual account, begins a new life. His spiritual birth, his "second birth," is inaugurated as he makes the transition from a life governed by this-worldly motivations to life within a

1. Caves, *vihāras* and more sophisticated shelters were considered as extra allowances.
2. Ibid., pp. 123-124.
3. Ibid., pp. 124-125.
4. Ibid., pp. 125-126.

community governed by and predicated upon *Dhamma*. It is only fitting that discipline and honesty are the final two issues brought to the newly ordained *bhikkhu*'s attention. For one's progress along the path to *nibbāna* and the maintenance of his good standing within the *bhikkhusaṅgha* will depend upon how well he reckons with volition and truth. They form the new basis for his new life apart from the world. The *bhikkhu* has been admitted to the community because he has qualified on the basis of meeting many exclusions formulated to secure the collective stature of the monastic order. His path is now the *bhikkhu* path, molded in the image of the mythical model, the Buddha, whose province it was to provide a paradigm for spiritual fruition through explication of *Dhamma*. Not to meet the prescriptions of the Buddha not only threatens the continued status of the *bhikkhu*, but brings criticism to the communal order as well. The newly ordained *bhikkhu* now shares in the heritage of the *bhikkhusaṅgha*, a heritage grounded in understanding the *Dhamma* made known by the Buddha and preserved and implemented through the inculcation of discipline.

Upasaṃpadā, therefore, represents the transition from an old orientation to a new orientation, a spiritual rebirth in which the individual is born anew into a new mode of being where ignorance has been dispelled and full understanding can be achieved. The new life is governed by the world view realized by the Buddha and preserved by the *Saṅgha* through the implementation of discipline.

The great importance attached to discipline by the *bhikkhusaṅgha* is further illustrated when we address ourselves to the manner in which the *Pāṭimokkha*, *Pavāraṇā* and *Kaṭhina* rites are depicted in subsequent chapters of the *Mahāvagga*. In those accounts, we shall see more clearly how discipline came to be cultically celebrated.

CHAPTER EIGHT

RITUAL EXPRESSIONS OF *BHIKKHU* DISCIPLINE : *PĀṬIMOKKHA*, *PAVĀRAṆĀ* AND *KAṬHINA*

Together, the *Upasampadā* and *Pāṭimokkha* comprise the most frequently celebrated and most important rituals of the *bhikkhu-saṅgha*. Essentially, the *Pāṭimokkha* recitation is a collective declaration of the monastic community's *parisuddhi* ("complete purity"). *Parisuddhi* can only be affirmed when all members of the monastic order are present, having gathered together on the appointed day (*Uposatha*) every two weeks to declare unfailing adherence to the over two hundred rules of discipline. We have already referred to the great importance attached to this ritual in connection with the earliest history of Buddhist monasticism.[1] In that discussion, we recounted the traditional understanding of the origins of this ritual as it is presented in the opening story of the second chapter of the *Mahāvagga*. As we remember, King Bimbisāra had requested that the Buddhists make known their *Dhamma* on *Uposatha*, as was the custom with other religious groups of the time. At first, the *bhikkhus* were silent; but when their silence was criticized by the laity, the Buddha instituted the practice of reciting all of the rules of discipline for that occasion. At least on this occasion, the reciting of the disciplinary rules is tantamount to propounding *Dhamma*.

The story which we have just summarized comprises the introductory literature to the *Mahāvagga*'s treatment of the *Pāṭimokkha* rite. What we must now do is press forward with our analysis to address the multiple regulations which follow this story. On the whole, these regulations reflect two basic concerns : that the local boundaries (*sīmā*) of each local *bhikkhusaṅgha* be strictly maintained and that every *bhikkhu* within those boundaries participate in the verbal recitation of the disciplinary rules. We must make apparent the significance of these concerns before we begin our analysis of the *Pavāraṇā* and *Kaṭhina* rites.

1. See pp. 37-40.

After the Buddha announces that all members who reside within the boundaries of residence must be present for the recitation of the disciplinary rules, a question arises as to what constitutes the boundaries. The Buddha's response is that the boundaries may be fixed by a variety of means, but that these boundaries need to be made known.[1] As usual, the *chabbaggiyas* find a way to confuse boundaries by overlapping them or overextending them.[2] In any case, the delineation of boundaries enables the *bhikkhus* of each residence to determine the respective areas from which all *bhikkhus* therein must gather for the recital. If any *bhikkhus* are sick or cannot attend for any valid reason, they are required to send a proxy in order for the rite to be validly executed.[3] Provisions are even made for *bhikkhus* with the residence who are being held captive or prisoner by secular authorities,[4] those who are not aware that the recital is being held,[5] those who are ignorant (incapable of conducting or participating in the recital),[6] those who are travelling through a residence or crossing boundaries during the day of the recital,[7] those who are mad,[8] those who are in danger and must leave their boundaried residences,[9] those who arrive late for the recital,[10] and for those *bhikkhus* who live in a residence that contains less than four members.[11] In addition, the proclamation of the order's *parisuddhi* through the recital could not be declared in the presence of *bhikkhunis*, novices, offenders of heinous crimes, those who have been expelled from the order, eunuchs, hermaphrodites, those who were on probation, or on any other day than *Uposatha*.[12]

We find a principle of separation at work here. The recitation of the *Pāṭimokkha* rules has become an internal affair which

1. *Book of Discipline* 4 : 137. Markers demarcating local *simās* were usually natural landmarks including hills, large rocks, large trees, rivers, etc.
2. Ibid., pp. 138-139 and 145-146.
3. Ibid., pp. 146-147, 150-152 and 158-160.
4. Ibid., p. 162.
5. Ibid., pp. 141 and 154-155.
6. Ibid., pp. 152-154 and 156-158.
7. Ibid., pp. 178-180.
8. Ibid., pp. 163-164.
9. Ibid., pp. 148-150.
10. Ibid., pp. 171-173.
11. Ibid., pp. 164-166.
12. Ibid., pp. 180-181.

establishes the identity of the *bhikkhusaṅgha vis-à-vis* the identity of others who are not fully accredited sojourners along the *bhikkhu* path of spirituality. The recital is an occasion whereby the collective order can affirm its adherence to discipline. However, these concerns for establishing rules for those who reside within the boundaries of their residences do not exhaust the significance of what is at work here.

In a stimulating article,[1] Akira Hirakawa stipulates that the idea of *Sammukhībhūta-saṅgha* is contingent upon the determination of boundaries, specifically the *Uposatha-sīmā* that is under consideration here.[2] Accordingly, the *Saṅgha* within each boundary was called a *Sammukhībhūta-saṅgha* "because this saṅgha was to be organized by the Bhikkhus 'existing face to face' within the boundary at one time."[3] The "existing face to face" description refers to the fact that all *bhikkhus* within each boundary were required to participate in all of the communal rituals.[4] In addition to the importance of boundaries for ritual life, we find that in *Mahāvagga* VIII (a *khandhaka* that focuses on the appropriate attire of *bhikkhus*), that all *bhikkhus* within a boundary were to receive an equal share of whatever robes were donated by the laity.[5] The same principle applies to the equal distribution of food for all members within the same boundary. Thus, boundaried *Saṅghas* enabled the *bhikkhu* community to administer communal ritual life and material concerns for each

1. Akira Hirakawa, "The Twofold Structure of the Buddhist Saṅgha," *Journal of the Baroda Institute* 16 (September, 1966) : 131-137.

2. Hirakawa notes that while the term "*Sammukhībhūta-saṅgha*," though "not found in the Pāli-uposatha-khandhaka, is used in the Chinese version of the Mahāsāṃghika vinaya..." Ibid., p. 133. He contends, however, that the same principle is at work in the Pāli version.

3. Ibid.

4. Hirakawa argues that this fact was also illustrated in *Cullavagga* XI, the account of the First Great Buddhist Council, wherein the 500 *bhikkhus* of Rājagaha determined that no other *bhikkhus* should enter inside their boundary while the council's deliberations were in progress. Ibid., pp. 133-134. The reasoning, apparently, was that not only was the internal business of the *Saṅgha* so important that all *bhikkhus* living within the boundary were required to attend, but also that the bhikkhus who resided outside the established boundaries were considered as potential disruptors.

5. *Book of Discipline* 4 : 441.

and every *bhikkhu.*[1] In that manner, all *bhikkhus* could be accounted for spiritually and materially.

However, in addition to the *Saṅgha* being determined by boundaries for the purpose of reciting the *Pāṭimokkha* rules and for the equal distribution of goods, we find another concept of *Saṅgha* at work that transcends the notion of boundaried communities. In *Mahāvagga* VIII, 27, 5 we read :

> On the death of a Bhikkhu, O Bhikkhus, the Saṅgha becomes the owner of his bowl and of his robes. But, now, those who wait upon the sick are of much service. I prescribe, O Bhikkhus, that the set of robes and bowls are to be assigned by the Saṅgha to them who have waited upon the sick. And whatever little property and small supply of requisites there may be, that is to be delivered by the Saṅgha that is present there; but whatever large quantity of property and large supply of a Bhikkhu's requisites there may be, that is not to be given away and not to be apportioned, but to belong to the Saṅgha of the four directions, those who have come in, and those who have not.[2]

We find this same mention of the "Saṅgha of the four directions" (Cātuddisasaṅgha) in *Cullavagga* VI, 1.[3] In that *khandhaka*, donations of *vihāras* and their furnishings by the laity are not given to the *Sammukhībhūta-saṅgha*, but to the *Cātuddisasaṅgha* instead. These properties belong to all *bhikkhus* of the present and all *bhikkhus* of the future. In other words, the permanent ownership of all significant properties belonged to the *Saṅgha*, but not exclusively to a particular *Sammukhībhūta-saṅgha*. By demarcating boundaries, the *Saṅgha* was able to administer the important recitation of the *Pāṭimokkha* rules properly and was also able to conduct daily affairs with regard to material goods of little consequence. However, ownership of anything that was of

1. Hirakawa points out that although the *Uposatha-sīmā* was the same boundary demarcated for food distribution and for ritual participation in the Pāli tradition, the Mahāsāṃghika, Dharmaguptaka, and Sarvāstivādin *Vinayas* contain special methods for the determination of food-sharing boundaries which are different from the *Uposatha-sīmā*. Hirakawa, "Two Fold," pp. 134-135. For an analysis of the spatial organization of contemporary monasteries, see Jacques Maquet, "Expressive Space and Theravāda Values," 1-21.

2. *Book of Discipline* 4 : 435-436.

3. Ibid., 5 : 204-206.

permanent quality belonged to the ideal *Saṅgha*, the universal *Saṅgha* of the past, present and future. *Now the disciplinary rules fall into that permanent category and as such become the property of the Cātuddisasaṅgha.* As Hirakawa rightly concludes :

> The Pāṭimokkha was laid down by the Buddha, but when he passed away the maintainer of the Pāṭimokkha was lost. The Saṅgha had to become the successor to the Buddha. But the Sammukhībhūta-saṅgha could not become the successor, because it had to obey the rules of the Pāṭimokkha. The Pāṭimokkha was held to be prior to the Sammukhībhūta-saṅgha. On the Buddha's passing away, it was determined that the Cātuddisasaṅgha should be the Representative of the Pāṭimokkha[1].

We have a two-fold structure of the *bhikkhusaṅgha* at work here. Significantly, that two-fold characteristic finds expression within the context of the *Pāṭimokkha* ritual. The delineation of several contemporary co-existing *saṅghas* through the demarcation of boundaried communities makes possible not only the efficacious transaction of the *Pāṭimokkha* ritual, but also the maintenance of the complete purity of the entire *bhikkhusaṅgha*, the *Cātuddisasaṅgha.* In other words, by regularly renewing the community's declaration of *parisuddhi* in matters of discipline, the *Cātuddisasaṅgha* could perpetually establish itself as the legitimate representative of the *Dhamma.* What binds the *Sammukhībhūta-saṅgha* to the *Cātuddisasaṅgha* is its proper execution of the *Pāṭimokkha* ritual. Boundaries functioned as practical tools that made such an administration of the ritual a possibility. Further, it provided each *Sammukhībhūta-saṅgha* with an 'opportunity to participate in something greater' than itself. The importance of executing this ritual in proper fashion no doubt accounts for the fact that after centuries of recitation, the disciplinary code remained incredibly similar in various recensions of the text.[2] But more importantly, the continued authoritative existence of the *Cātuddisasaṅgha* was dependent upon each boundaried community properly making its declaration of collective and complete purity.

1. Hirakawa, "Two Fold," p. 136.
2. See our chart on page 40 of chapter 3.

There is one more aspect about the *Pāṭimokkha* ritual that we have not commented upon previously and which we find to be very important to our discussions. That aspect becomes evident when we remember that the detailed regulations for the execution of the ritual require that all members who reside within the same boundary are physically present and verbally enumerate all of the disciplinary rules of the *Pāṭimokkha* code. After each section of the code is recited by all of the participants, the "learned and competent" elder leading the recital asks all members present if they are pure with regard to the rules just cited. By their silence, the *bhikkhus* acknowledge their purity. However, each member has verbally chanted in unison every single disciplinary precept before being governed by the elder. Furthermore, there must be absolutely no doubt in the minds of all *bhikkhus* that they are indeed pure. If a *bhikkhu* has been guilty of an offence, that offence must be confessed ahead of time. If an offence is concealed and later becomes known, severe penalties are enforced, i.e., *Pārājika* 4. If all *bhikkhus* within the same boundary are guilty of offences, they must send for a *bhikkhu* from another residence to conduct the recitation.[1] But the interesting point here is, that, as we mentioned earlier, the expression of one's inner state is communicated through three modes : body, speech, and thought. The *Pāṭimokkha* recitation is designed to express the inward purity of the *Saṅgha* through those same modes. All *bhikkhus* are required to be physically (bodily) gathered together as one. They are required to chant each and every disciplinary rule in unison. And, they are required to have absolutely no doubt in their minds with regard to their own behavior in relation to each rule. Thus, proper execution of the *Pāṭimokkha* ritual expresses the pure quality of the inward state of the collective community *in toto* through body, speech and thought. It is this unified, collective expression of purity that acknowledges, legitimates, and perpetuates the *bhikkhusaṅgha* as the authentic bearer of the spiritual path that was articulated by the Buddha. Moreover, it recalls and maintains the relationship between the contemporary boundaried *Saṅgha* and the "*Saṅgha* of the four quarters." It is, in fact, the essential expression of *bhikkhu* communal life and spirituality that defines the identity

1. *Book of Discipline* 4 : 166-171.

of the order : it ties the boundaried community to its "pristine past," celebrates its contemporary success and charisma, and makes possible the continuation of its mission in the future. For the Buddhist *bhikkhus*, the *Pāṭimokkha* ritual is a formal expression of the ideal married to the real. It is the cultic celebration of the principle of the Buddha's path : discipline—that feature of self-effort that defies and arrests conditioning.

When we come to the *Mahāvagga*'s treatment of the *Pavāraṇā*, we are struck by the functional similarity it bears to the *Pāṭimokkha* recitation. In comparing these two rituals, I. B. Horner has observed that

> The recital of the Pāṭimokkha was to "to remove" offences, by confessing them, during the nine dry months of the year; the Invitation [Pavāraṇā] was to remove any offences that monks had committed during the three wet months [vassa], and would help them to aim at grasping discipline.[1]

Instead of being held every two weeks, the *Pavāraṇā*, like the *Kaṭhina* rite, was held annually at the end of *vassa* retreat. Individual *bhikkhus* were "invited" to confess transgressions against the disciplinary code at this time.

Although the *Pavāraṇā* is a ritual that expresses purity with regard to the disciplinary code and the practical implementation of *Dhamma* in the same vein as the *Pāṭimokkha* rite, there remain crucial differences between the two. Instead of the collective *bhikkhusaṅgha* reciting all of the disciplinary precepts in unison and declaring adherence, as is the case in the *Pāṭimokkha* rite, each *bhikkhu* is invited to crouch before the assembly of gathered members and petition his fellow *bhikkhu* brothers to judge his conduct according to the rules of discipline. If the crouching *bhikkhu* has been guilty of an offence, he is charged by one of his brothers with the transgression. Should he be guilty of the offence, the matter is settled according to the penalties made explicit within in the *Suttavibhaṅga* section of the *Vinaya*. Unlike the *Pāṭimokkha* ritual in which transgressions are confessed ahead of time before the *bhikkhusaṅgha*'s recitation of the disciplinary rules, a violation of the rules is not voluntarily given by the *bhikkhu* under scrutinization. Rather, a transgression is pointed out by *bhikkhus* who have witnessed the violation. Like

1. Horner, *Introduction to Book of Discipline* 4 : xvii; brackets mine.

the murmuring laity who we have already noted in *Suttavibhaṅga* literature, other *bhikkhus* aid in checking the behavior of their *bhikkhu* brothers in the *Pavāraṇā* ritual context. In other words, whereas the preliminary rubrics of the *Pāṭimokkha* encourage *bhikkhus* to examine their own personal behavior, the *Pavāraṇā* encourages *bhikkhus* to evaluate each other's conduct. Although both rituals are designed to maintain *parisuddhi*, the *Pāṭimokkha* is clearly a more liturgical rite while the *Pavāraṇā* occasion serves as a type of court of law.

By examining the dynamics of the *Pavāraṇā* occasion, we can go beyond understanding the *Pavāraṇā* as a ritual that only cultically expresses the community's collective adherence to discipline. Moreover, we have an opportunity to observe how determinations were made with regard to violations of the disciplinary code. In so doing, we can continue to gain insight into how the early Buddhist community perceived the nature of undisciplined and disciplined actions.

The *Mahāvagga*'s prescriptions for the *Pavāraṇā* ritual are found in *Mahāvagga* IV. The account begins with a story that leads up to the point where the Buddha decides to initiate *Pavāraṇā* in order to further harmonious interaction during the rainy season when *bhikkhus* lived together communally.

> I allow, monks, monks who have kept the rains to invite [each other] in regard to three matters : what has been seen or heard or suspected. That will be what is suitable for you in regard to one another, a removal of offences, an aiming at grasping the discipline.[1]

The Buddha is then depicted as outlining the procedure for determining the legitimacy of an accusation with the following proclamation :

> In case, O monks, one monk on the day of Pavāraṇā inhibits the Pavāraṇā of another monk : then if the other monks know with regard to that inhibiting monk : "This venerable brother is of pure conduct in his deeds and in his words and with regard to his means of livelihood, he is clever, learned, and able to give an explanation when he is questioned," let them say to him : "If you inhibit, friend, the Pavāraṇā of this monk, on what account do you inhibit it, on account of a moral

1. *Book of Discipline* 4 : 211.

transgression, or on account of a transgression against the rules of conduct, or on account of heresy ?"[1]

The accusing *bhikkhu* is then asked to explain his understanding of what entails a moral transgression, a transgression against the rules of conduct, and a transgression that constitutes heresy. We are then presented with a series of manipulated questions and answers with regard to the nature of moral transgressions, transgressions against the rules of conduct, and heretical teachings. If one *bhikkhu* charges another with a moral transgression, he must state that he has seen, heard or suspected[2] that the *bhikkhu* in question has violated a *pārājika* or *saṅghādisesa* precept. If one *bhikkhu* charges another with a transgression against one of the rules of conduct, he must state that he has seen, heard or suspected that the *bhikkhu* in question has violated one of the *pāṭidesaniya*, *pācittiya*, *thullacaya* or *dukkaṭa* prescriptions. The latter two (*thullacaya*— grave offence"; *dukkaṭa*—"wrong-doing") are judgments against unsuitable behavior with regard to any of the *Vinaya* rules, but penalties are less severe than the ones handed down for *pārājika* and *saṅghādisesa* violations. If a charge is brought by one *bhikkhu* against another that concerns heresy, the specific point of errant doctrine must be identified by the accusing *bhikkhu*.

From this description of the *Pavāraṇā* procedure, several important observations can be made. The first is that in order to bring a charge against another *bhikkhu*, the accusing *bhikkhu* must be thoroughly familiar with all of the disciplinary precepts. If his charge is found to be unwarranted, he is found to be guilty of a *dukkaṭa* offence himself. Charges were therefore taken very seriously and had to be substantiated by evidence. As the description of the *Pavāraṇā* procedure notes, an offence must be seen, heard or suspected. That is, an offence against the *Vinaya* rules is always expressed through bodily, verbal or mental modes of expression. These external modes of expression were

1. *Book of Discipline* 4 : 225.

2. If a *bhikkhu* brings a charge against another *bhikkhu* on the basis of what he has "suspected," he must answer the following questions : What did you suspect ? How did you suspect ? When did you suspect ? Where did you suspect ? These primary questions are then followed by a battery of other more specific questions in order to completely identify the legitimacy of the charge. See ibid., p. 227.

considered, as we have noted repeatedly, to be manifestations of the inward condition of the *bhikkhu.* Thus, if a charge of breaking one of the *Vinaya* rules is sustained by evidence based upon the observation of bodily, verbal or mental expression, then the transgressing *bhikkhu* is identified as one who has failed to sustain a disciplined inward demeanor, unless he can prove that his transgressing act was unintentional.

The second observation that is apparent from the description of the *Pavāraṇā* procedure is that the disciplinary rules are not referred to as a whole as "morality" or "ethics." Only the *pārājikas* and *saṅghādisesas* are referred to as such.

Again, we have discovered that the disciplinary rules involve much more than merely an elaboration of *sīla.* Rather, taken as a whole, they must be considered as the effective implementation of a mindset which has embraced the world view made explicit in the teachings of the Four Noble Truths. Although ethical notions figure heavily, they do not comprise the whole of what is involved in discipline.

Finally, there is the fact that once the *Pavāraṇā* has taken place and corrective procedures have been meted out to offenders, the *bhikkhusaṅgha* is considered to be collectively pure with regard to the disciplinary rules. That is particularly significant in the light of the fact that the *Pavāraṇā* is held immediately preceding the *Kaṭhina* ceremony. As the *Kaṭhina* ceremony represents an affair in which the laity express their admiration to the *bhikkhusaṅgha*, the *Pavāraṇā* transactions serve to confirm the deserving status of the *bhikkhu* community. In one sense, it serves as a preliminary event for the *Kaṭhina* ritual context.

As is characteristic of the *Vinaya*'s treatment of important facets of *bhikkhu* communal life and rituals, an extensive textual treatment outlines the appropriate procedures and rules that govern the proper enactment of the *Kaṭhina* rite.[1] As we are now not so concerned with the nature of these many details, we can proceed to describe the *Kaṭhina* rite in cursory fashion. A worthy *bhikkhu* (one who has been declared to have adhered to all of the disciplinary rules during *vassa*) is selected to receive

1. *Book of Discipline* 4 : 351-378. For an extensive consideration of these details, see Heinz Bechert, "Some Remarks on the Kaṭhina Rite." *Journal of the Bihar Research Society* 54 (1968) : 319-329.

the *Kaṭhina* cloth from the laity on behalf of the rest of the *bhikkhus* in residence. That especially selected *bhikkhu* then says :

> This Kaṭhina cloth has become the property of the Saṅgha. If the Saṅgha is ready, hand over the Kaṭhina cloth to such and such a Bhikkhu to spread out the Kaṭhina.[1]

The "spreading out" refers to the work entailed in the making of new robes to be distributed among the *bhikkhus* of a boundaried residence. The construction of new robes must take place within one day and if needed, all *bhikkhus* can help in the process of making the new robes according to prescribed lengths. The robes are then washed, dyed and dried in the sun.

The meaning of the *Kaṭhina* ceremony can be partially ascertained if we rely exclusively upon the story in *Mahāvagga* VII, 1, that introduces the practice.[2] In that story, we are told how group of thirty *bhikkhus*, after observing *vassa*, were on their way to visit the Buddha at Sāvatthi. On their way, they were drenched with rain and forced to wade through swamps. Consequently, their robes appeared unkempt. The Buddha thus prescribed the giving of new robe material by the laity to the *bhikkhusaṅgha*. From this story, we can correctly deduce that the institution of the *Kaṭhina* rite evolved out of concern for the appearance of the *bhikkhus*. Since the *bhikkhus* attending this communal ritual were considered to be pure with regard to disciplinary conduct (and thus to possess a disciplined inward disposition), the giving of material for new robes symbolizes the laity's desire that *bhikkhus* appear outwardly pure as well.

Be that as it may, the *Kaṭhina* rite also provides an occasion whereupon the laity can demonstrate its appreciation to *bhikkhus* who are worthy of support. As Alec Robertson has pointed out :

> One great advantage of the Kaṭhina-ceremony is that it brings together the bhikkhus and the lay-devotees. The bhikkhus receive from the laity the requisites of the monk life which are necessary for their physical well-being, and at the same time, promote their spiritual progress on the path to deliverance. The bhikkhus reciprocate the liberality of the laity by providing the latter with spiritual nutriment for their well-being here

1. *Book of Discipline* 4 : 353.
2. Ibid., pp. 351-358.

and hereafter. This mutual inter-dependence of the Saṅgha and laity is essential for the strength, the unity, the solidarity and the longevity of the Buddha-Sâsana.[1]

Robertson is pointing to the fact that both lay and *bhikkhu* factions of the Buddhist community benefit from the reciprocal relationship that is formally acknowledged within the *Kaṭhina* rite. Laity gain merit by providing the most important material goods to the most auspicious field of merit. A pure and unified *bhikkhusaṅgha* is required in the transaction for it to result in a meritorious reward for the laity. On the other hand, *bhikkhus* gain the material necessities they need in order to continue with their "spiritual pursuits." In contrast to the *Upasampadā*, *Pāṭimokkha* and *Pavāraṇā* rites which involve only the *bhikkhu* membership of the community, the *Kaṭhina* rite allows for the participation of both *bhikkhu* and lay segments of the community. In the other rituals we have just mentioned, the *bhikkhus* declare their purity and thereby their authority in spiritual matters; but in the *Kaṭhina* rite, the laity are given the opportunity to recognize that special status of the *bhikkhus*. The *Kaṭhina* rite is to the collective *Saṅgha* what the act of almsgiving is to the individual *bhikkhu* : a symbolic act recognizing the special status of the Buddhist holy man. Thus, the significance of adhering to discipline is two-fold in this context : not only does discipline further the spiritual pursuit of the individual *bhikkhu* and confirm the special status of the *bhikkhusaṅgha* as the spiritual virtuosos of the Buddhist community, but it also provides the laity with an occasion to gain merit for their own quests to gain a better rebirth.

These observations with regard to ritual expression within the *Vinayapiṭaka* reflect the high premium placed upon the importance of adhering to the prescriptions of discipline that are traditionally attributed to the Buddha. The religious ethos of the *Vinaya* is characterized by a judicious concern for the individual *bhikkhu*, the *bhikkhusaṅgha* and the lay supporters of the community. From the perspective of the early Buddhist followers, adherence to discipline and participation in the religious ritual life of the community enabled a structure of relationships to be sustained. When complete purity (*parisuddhi*) was declared, the

1. Alec Robertson, *The Triple Gem and the Uposatha* (Colombo : The Colombo Apothecaries Co., 1971), p. 118.

eternal presence of the Buddha's *Dhamma* was formally affirmed. The *bhikkhusaṅgha* could thus legitimately claim to embody the Buddha's teachings and claim to fulfil its role as the successor to the Buddha's authority in matters of spirituality. Such claims had to be carefully guarded and could only be maintained by a rigorously defined, properly enforced and publicly acknowledged system of discipline.

CHAPTER NINE

CONCLUSION

The Buddhism envisaged within the *Vinayapiṭaka* is a religion of the individual and a religion of the community. Discipline is understood to be of vital necessity for gaining the goal of *nibbāna* and for maintaining the collective identity of the *bhikkhusaṅgha*.

Throughout the pages of the *Vinayapiṭaka*, the two terms *Dhamma* and *Vinaya* are constantly referred to in conjunction with one another. A number of followers of the Buddha are repeatedly identified as experts in the two. From the point of view of our text, the two terms cannot be regarded as two separate aspects of the Buddhist path. But rather, a rudimentary relationship exists between cognitive realization and practical expression.

The *Cullavagga* relates that immediately after the death of the Buddha, five hundred of his followers gathered together and after some hesitation recited the Buddha's verses on *Dhamma* and *discipline*. The historicity of this account is not of central importance to this discussion. However, the *Vinaya*'s account of the First Great Buddhist Council signals a primary function of the *bhikkhusaṅgha* : it is a preserver of *Dhamma*. Adherence to discipline preserves the *Dhamma* in practice and legitimates the status of the monastic community. This is precisely the view that emerges from the text, a view that we have attempted to outline in the two previous chapters. In this concluding chapter, however, we need to underscore the importance of reciting *Dhamma* and *Vinaya* and the implications that this practice raises for viewing the structure of the Buddhist community.

E. W. Adhikaram has surveyed the commentaries of the Pāli canon while attempting to determine the nature and origin of the *bhāṇaka* (reciter) tradition. He argues that the beginnings of the *bhāṇaka* tradition are ancient and responsible for the transmission of sacred scripture from India to Ceylon. As he draws upon the *Cullavagga* account of the legendary First Council, he recognizes a division of labor among the *bhāṇakas* and proceeds to describe how various *bhikkhus* were responsible for the transmission of portions of sacred scripture as the *bhāṇaka* tradition evolved through time:

> With regard to the three divisions of the Canon: the Sutta, the Vinaya and the Abhidhamma, we find that those who recited and handed them down were not known by the name *Bhāṇaka* but were designated Suttantikā, Vinayadharā and Abhidhammika respectively. Dhammadharā was another name for Suttantikā. The Buddha himself was considered the first Abhidhammikā. Those who studied and recited the Commentaries were called *Aṭṭhakathikā*. Besides these there were the *Tipiṭakā* (those versed in the three *Piṭakas*) and the Catunikāyikā (those versed in the four Nikāyas). Again, there were those who studied all the three Piṭakas but specialized in one Nikāya. . . It is necessary to note here that being a Bhāṇaka of a particular section of the Canon only meant that a person in question made a special study of that portion and did not imply an ignorance or neglect of other sections of the Piṭakas.[1]

Yet, Adhikaram carefully notes that some factionalism did occur within monasticism as the result of this division of labor among the *bhāṇakas*. As a matter of fact, it seems that often one portion of canonical writings is emphasized over others by certain groups within a religious tradition. In Protestant Christianity, the Pauline epistles provide a familiar example. In Mahāyāna Buddhism, particular *sūtras* were often regarded as the chief expression and source of truth. And, it is not surprising that *Vinayadharās* would make special appeals to *Vinaya* literature in order to legitimate a certain view, or that *Abhidhammikās* would make the same kind of appeals to the *Abhidhamma* literature. Furthermore, the existence and popularity of these various *bhāṇaka* traditions are probably partially responsible for the fact that Anuruddha, Sāriputta, Ananda, Mahākassapa and Upāli (all of whom were regarded as the first reciters of certain texts) were so highly venerated in developing Buddhist lore. *Avādāna* literature is replete with legends that lionize these figures. Nevertheless, the emergence of this mild form of sectarianism in no way precludes the overall function of the *bhāṇakas* (and hence

1. E. W. Adhikaram, *Early History of Buddhism in Ceylon* (Colombo: D. S. Puswella, 1946), pp. 24-32.

one important function of the *bhikkhusaṅgha*) : to preserve the *Dhamma* realized and made known by the Buddha.[1]

Hearing *Dhamma* preached or recited by *bhikkhus* was understood to be an act of meritorious consequence by the laity. Indeed, their chief source of *Dhamma* was none other than the sermons and scriptural recitations of the *bhikkhu*. To insure that these presentations of *Dhamma* were carried out forthrightly, we have noted that a good number of disciplinary rules designate special conditions for *Dhamma* presentations and dictate the behavior expected of a *bhikkhu* on those occasions. Given these lines of *Dhamma* transmission, a structure of relationships constitutive of the Buddhist community begins to emerge.

The *Dhamma* was realized by the Buddha who transmitted it to his disciples. These disciples remembered and codified his teachings and kept them alive through the *bhāṇaka* vocation. The *Dhamma* was thus preserved for *bhikkhus* of every age who in turn became the chief sources of *Dhamma* for the laity. The *bhikkhu-saṅgha* was able to legitimate its role as a refuge unto the laity precisely because it represented that portion of the community that maintained the practice of *Dhamma* through adhering to discipline. By means of the chart below, the structure of the Buddhist community according to these considerations is depicted:

Dhamma → Buddha → Chief Disciples → Bhāṇakas (textual traditions)
↓
bhikkhus
↓
laity

Yet, we cannot forget that this schematization reflects the view of the Buddhist community that surfaces as a result of considering thoroughly monastic sources. If we had access to the same kinds of sources that reflect the manner in which the structure of the community was viewed by the laity, it is quite possible that the relationships would be reconstructed in a different way. However, we simply lack adequate sources to responsibly indicate how the laity would have assessed the situation. On the other hand, we do find some helpful hints within the Pāli literature which indicate that the pattern of relationships were more complex than we have just depicted them to be.

1. E. W. Adhikaram, *Early History of Buddhism in Ceylon* (Colombo : D. S. Puswella, 1946), p. 25

A brief passage in the *Mahāparinibbāna Sutta* alludes to an important practice among the laity which had prodigious implications for the history of Buddhist piety. This *sutta* focuses upon the last months of Gotama's career preceding his death. As it is part of the *Dīgha Nikāya*, it represents a solidly *bhikkhu* perspective. The passage that we are concerned with occurs in the midst of a dialogue that the Buddha is conducting with Ānanda :

> 'What are we to do, Lord, with the remains of the Tathāgata ?'
>
> 'Hinder not yourselves, Ānanda, by honoring the remains of the Tathāgata. Be zealous, I beseech you, Ānanda, in your own behalf ! Be earnest, be zealous, be intent on your own good ! There are wise men, Ānanda, among the nobles, among the heads of houses, who are firm believers in the Tathāgata; and they will do due honor to the remains of the Tathāgata.'
>
> 'What should be done, Lord, with the remains of the Tathāgata ?'
>
> 'As men treat the remains of a king of kings, so, Ānanda, should they treat the remains of a Tathāgata.'
>
> 'And how, Lord, do they treat the remains of a king of kings?'
>
> 'They wrap the body of the king of kings, Ānanda, in a new cloth. When that is done, they wrap it in a carded cotton wool. When that is done, they wrap it in a new cloth,—and so on till they have wrapped the body in five hundred successive layers of both kinds. Then they place the body in an oil vessel of iron, and cover that close up with another vessel of iron. Then they build a funeral pile of all kinds of perfumes, and burn the body of the king of kings. And then at the four cross-roads, they erect a dāgaba to the king of kings. This, Ānanda, is the way in which they treat the remains of the king of kings.
>
> 'And as they treat the remains of the king of kings, so, Ānanda, should they treat the remains of the Tathāgata. At the four cross-roads a dāgaba should be erected to the Tathāgata. And whosoever shall place there garlands or perfumes or paint, or make a salutation there, or become in its presence calm in heart—that shall long be to them a profit and a joy.'[1]

1. E. W. Adhikaram,, *Early History of Buddhism in Ceylon* (Colombo : D. S. Puswella, 1946), p. 32.

It is very clear from this passage that *stūpa* worship was not advocated by the Buddha for *bhikkhu* followers, since Ānanda represents the *bhikkhu* presence in this *sutta*. However, we have been told that the practice of *stūpa* worship is profitable for householders. And since we know that the date of this text is very ancient, we have some assurance that the practice of *stūpa* worship occurred during the time period with which we have been so concerned throughout this book.

The fact that the Buddha reportedly gave the responsibility to the laity for taking care of his remains is very suggestive. As the *bhikkhus* were charged with maintaining the *Dhammakāya* of their master, so were the laity charged with the maintenance of the *rupakāya* (the relics of the Buddha). Frank Reynolds, in commenting upon the nature of these Buddhaic charges says that

> There is a strong body of evidence which suggests that during the canonical period this division both grounded and reflected the realities of life in the Buddhist community. The study, recitation, and interpretation of the remembered teachings provided a major focal point of identity and life in the early Buddhist order of *bhikkhus*, and particularly after the time of Asoka, the reliquary *stūpas* and the cult associated with them came to play an increasingly important role as the prime focal point of Buddhist identity and life among the laity. Moreover, in the period between the closing of the canon and the translation of the Sinhalese commentaries into Pāli, the two legacies came to be referred to as the Buddha's *dhammakāya* on the one hand and his *rupakāya* on the other.[1]

Thus, as the *bhikkhus* preserved and celebrated *Dhamma* and discipline (the teachings of the Buddha), the laity celebrated the life and presence of the Buddha.

Keeping this important point in mind, the relationship between the laity and the three refuges of Buddhism becomes clear. While the laity venerated the *bhikkhusaṅgha* because of the special relationship between the monastic community and the preservation of the *Dhamma*, they also venerated the Buddha, and for the same reason that they venerated the *Saṅgha* : the Buddha

1. Frank Reynolds, "The Several Bodies of Buddha : Reflections on a Neglected Aspect of Theravada Tradition," *History of Religions* 17 (May, 1977) : 376.

realized *Dhamma* and then proceeded out of his compassion to make it known through his own exemplary life and teachings. The diagram below indicates the structure of this network of relationships :

Dhamma → Buddha → Disciples → Bhāṇakas (textual traditions)
↓ ↓
stūpa worship ——→ laity ←—— bhikkhus

In each case, our diagrams indicate the residual importance of *Dhamma*. And the fact that we have endeavored throughout our discussions to link *Dhamma* and *Vinaya* as two inclusive aspects of the same path leading to *nibbāna* brings the importance of discipline for the monastic community again to light. The Saṅgha's status as one of three Buddhist refuges is based upon its cultivation of *Dhamma* in practice and its role in preserving the *Dhamma* for all in the present and in the future. Meeting the prescriptions of the disciplinary code and cultically celebrating such adherence symbolize the fulfilling of that role on the level of the individual *bhikkhu* and on the level of the collective monastic community.

The ethos of discipline, when considered as a soteriological means, is characterized by the belief that an individual, through insight and effort, can conquer the fetters of existence that perpetuate a suffering condition. This is a path that is primarily one of self-effort. For no matter how much refuge may be taken in the *Tri-ratna* (Triple Gem), the individual must, on his own accord, still the fires of ego-oriented passions. It is exactly this ethos of discipline that separates the path to *nibbāna* from other soteriological traditions in the "higher" religions of the world. The path of discipline involves no restoration from a fallen status to a state of grace. There is no intervening savior figure to accomplish the humanly impossible. Nowhere do we find the doctrine of predestination contemplated. There is an absence of contemplating the nature of deity, or meeting a "high God" face to face. Thus, there is no experience of *mysterium tremendum* or *mysterium fascinosum*. There is no summons to experience the one without a second, to gain union with an ontological essence of being. For Buddhism is not a soteriological tradition that can be understood in the same vein as Christianity, Judaism, Hinduism or Islam. Rather, as it is envisaged within the *Vinayapiṭaka*, it is pre-eminently a religion of disciplined effort where no appeal is made to an outside intervening power or to an all-pervasive Being. It is a religion in which each individual forges his own spiritual destiny on the basis of how well he comprehends the nature of reality and acts on the basis of that comprehension. It is an ideology and a practice with reference to ultimate transformation. When the insight and awareness facilitated by an understanding of *Dhamma* are realized, and the *Vinaya* strategy of action is resolutely pursued, then the final goal is attained.

> As the vast ocean, O bhikkhus, is pregnant with one taste, the taste of salt, so also, O bhikkhus, is this Dhamma and Discipline pregnant with only one taste : the taste of deliverance.[1]
>
> —Cullavagga IX. i. 4.

1. *Book of Discipline* 5 : 331-332.

APPENDIX

The following tables represent our attempt to relate minor rules of discipline to the concerns of the *pārājikas*.[1]

Table 1
PĀRĀJIKA I

	II	III	IV	V	VI	VII	VIII
	1 2	1 2	5 6	6 7 24	1 2	1 2 3 4 5 6	—
	3 4			25 26 27		7 8 9 10 11 12	
	5			28 29 30		13 14 15 16 17 18	
				43 44 45		19 20 21 22 23 24	
				67		25 26	
Totals :	5	2	2	13	2	26	—

Grand Total :[*] 47 + 1 *pārājika* = 48 major and minor rules relating to the issue of sexual improprieties of conditions that might lead to such.

[*]The fact that we have attempted to be very liberal in our association of these rules is demonstrated by virtue of the fact that Pachow lists only twenty-five rules (*Sarvāstivādin*) as relating to matters with the opposite sex. Tachibana says that he finds only twenty-one in this regard. See Tachibana, *Ethics of Buddhism*, p. 142.

Table 2
PĀRĀJIKA II

	II	III	IV	V	VI	VII	VIII
	—	—	3 7 8 9 10 11	24 31 33 34	3 4	—	—
			12 13 14 15 16 17	35 36 37 38			
			18 19 20 21 22 23	39 40 46 47			
			24 25 26 27 28 30	58 59 60 66			
				82 84 86 87			
				88 89 90 91			
				92			
Totals :	0	0	24	25	2	0	0

Grand Total : 51 + 1 *pārājika* = 52 major and minor rules relating in some fashion to the issue of "taking what is not given," or for the purpose at hand, to the issue of "having in possession that which is not allowed."

1. Column II refers to the class of *saṅghādisesa* rules, III refers to *aniyata* rules, IV to *nissaggiya* rules, V to *pācittiya* rules, VI to *pāṭidesanīya* rules, VII to *sekhiya* rules, and VIII to the seven *adhikaraṇasamatha* ways of settling a dispute.

Table 3
PĀRĀJIKA III

II	III	IV	V	VI	VII	VIII
6 7	—	—	10 11 12 13 14	—	—	—
			15 16 19 20 48			
			49 50 56 61 62			
			74 75			
Totals :						
2	0	0	17	0	0	0

Grand Total : 19+1 *pārājika*=20 major and minor rules that relate to the issue of killing.

Table 5
PĀRĀJIKA IV

II	III	IV	V	VI	VII	VIII
8 9 11	—	—	1 2 3 4	—	—	—
			63 64 65 68			
			69 70 76 79			
			80 81			
Totals :						
3	0	0	14	0	0	0

Grand Total : 17+1 *pārājika*=18 major and minor rules relating to the act of lying in a general fashion.

In tabulating our results, we see that 139 out of 227 Pāli disciplinary rules can be related to the central concerns of the *pārājikas*.

SELECTED BIBLIOGRAPHY

Translations and Transliterations of Buddhist Texts

The Vinaya Piṭikaṃ. Edited with an Introduction by Hermann Oldenberg. 5 vols. London : Williams and Norgate, 1879.

The Book of Discipline (*Vinayapiṭaka*). Translated with Introductions by I. B. Horner. 5 vols. Sacred Books of the Buddhists. Vols. 10, 11, 13, 14, and 20. London : Oxford University Press, 1938-52.

Vinaya Texts. Translated with an Introduction to T. W. Rhys Davids and Hermann Oldenberg. 3 vols. Sacred Books of the East. Vols. 13, 17, and 20. London : Oxford University Press, 1881.

Aṭṭhasālini by Buddhaghoṣa. Edited and translated by P. V. Bapat and R. D. Badekar. Poona : Bhandarkar Oriental Research Institute, 1942.

The Book of Kindred Sayings (*Saṃyutta Nikāya*). Translated by C. A. F. Rhys Davids and F. L. Woodward. 5 vols. Pāli Text Society Translation Series, Nos. 7, 10, 13, 14, and 16. London : Oxford University Press, 1917-30.

The Book of Gradual Sayings (*Aṅguttara Nikāya*). Translated by F. L. Woodward and E. M. Hare. 5 vols. Pāli Text Society Translation Series, Nos. 22, 24-27. London : Oxford University Press, 1930-36.

The Middle Length Sayings (*Majjhima Nikāya*). Translated by I. B. Horner. 3 vols. Pāli Text Society Translation Series Nos. 29-31. London : Luzac and Company, 1954-59.

Dialogues of the Buddha (*Dīgha Nikāya*). Translated and edited by T. W. Rhys Davids and C. A. F. Rhys Davids. 3 vols. Sacred Books of the Buddhists. Vols. 2-4. London : Luzac and Company, 1899-1921.

Visuddhimagga (*The Path of Purification*) by Buddhaghoṣa. Translated by Bhikkhu Nyāṇamoli. 2 vols. Berkeley : Shambhala Publications, 1976.

Milindapañha (*The Questions of King Milinda*). Translated by T. W. Rhys Davids. 2 vols. Sacred Books of the East. Vols. 34-35. London : Oxford University Press, 1894; reprint ed., New Delhi : Motilal Banarsidass, 1965.

General Literature

Adhikaram, E. W. *Early History of Buddhism in Ceylon*. Colombo : D. S. Puswella, 1946.

Bareau, Andre. *Recherches sur la biographie du Buddha dans le Sūtrapitika et les Vinayapitika Anciens*. Publications de L'Ecole Francaise d'Extreme-Orient. No. 53. Paris : Ecole Francaise d'Extreme-Orient, 1963.

———. *Les premiers conciles bouddhiques*. Paris : Presses Universitaires, 1955.

Bechert, Heinz. "Some Remarks on the Kathina Rite." *Journal of the Bihar Research Society* 54 (1968) : 319-29.

Bhattacharya, B. C. *The History of Sarnath or the Cradle of Buddhism*. Benares : Ramashwar Patak, 1924.

Bush, Richard. "Foundations for Ethics in the Sacred Scriptures of Ancient Hinduism and Early Buddhism." Ph.D. dissertation, The University of Chicago, 1960.

Chang, Kun. *A Comparative Study of the Kaṭhinavastu*. Indo-Iranian Monographs No. 1. s'Gravenhage : Mouton and Company, 1957.

Conze, Edward. *Buddhism : Its Essence and Development*. New York : Harper and Row, Publishers, 1959.

———. *Buddhist Thought in India*. London : George Allen and Unwin, Ltd., 1962; reprint ed., Ann Arbor : University of Michigan Press, 1973.

De, Goukaldas. *Democracy in the Early Buddhist Saṃgha*. Calcutta : Calcutta University Press, 1955.

Demieville, Paul. "A propos du concile de Vaisali." *Toung Pao* 40 (1951) : 239-96.

Dutt, Nalinaksha. *Buddhist Sects in India*. Calcutta : K. L. Mukhopadyay, 1970.

———. *Early History and Spread of Buddhism and the Buddhist Schools*. Calcutta Oriental Series No. 14. London : Luzac and Company, 1925.

———. *Early Monastic Buddhism*. Calcutta : Calcutta Oriental Book Agency, 1960.

Dutt, Nalinaksha. "The Second Buddhist Council." *Indian Historical Quarterly* 35 (March 1959) : 45-56.

Dutt, Sukumar. *The Buddha and Five After-Centuries.* London: Luzac and Company, 1957.

———. *Buddhist Monks and Monasteries of India: Their History and Their Contribution to Indian Culture.* London : George Allen and Unwin, Ltd., 1962.

———. *Early Buddhist Monachism.* London : Kegan Paul, Trench, Trübner and Co., 1924.

Eliade, Mircea. *No Souvenirs.* New York : Harper and Row, Publishers, 1977.

Encyclopedia of Buddhism. 1964 ed., s.v. "Arahant."

Encyclopedia of Religion and Ethics. 1914 ed., s.v. "Karma," by Louis de La Vallée Poussin.

Foucher, Alfred. *The Life of the Buddha According to the Texts and Monuments of India.* Translated by Simone B. Boas. Middletown, Conn. : Wesleyan University Press, 1963.

Franke, R. O. "The Buddhist Councils at Rājagaha and Vesali as Alleged in *Cullavagga* XI, XII." *Journal of the Pāli Text Society* 8 (1908) : 1-80.

Frauwallner, Erich. *The Earliest Vinaya and the Beginnings of Buddhist Literature.* Serie Orientale No. 8. Rome : Instituto Italiano per il Medio ed Estremo Oriente, 1956.

Gombrich, Richard. *Precept and Practice : Traditional Buddhism in the Rural Highlands of Ceylon.* London : Oxford University Press, 1971.

Gunther, Herbert. "Die Buddhistisch Kosmogonie." *Zeitschrift der deutchen morgenlandischen Gesellschaft* 98 (January 1944) : 44-83.

Hirakawa, Akira. "The Rise of Mahāyāna Buddhism and its Relation to the Worship of Stūpas." *Memoirs of the Research Department of the Toyo Bunko* 22 (1963) : 57-106.

———. *A Study of the Vinayapiṭaka.* Tokyo : Sankibo-Busshorin, 1960.

———. "The Two-fold Structure of the Buddhist Saṁgha." *Journal of the Baroda Institute* 16 (September, 1966) : 131-37.

Hofinger, M. *Etude sur le concile de Vaiśālī.* Louvain : Bureau de Museon, 1946.

Horner, I. B. *The Basic Position of Sila.* Colombo : The Bauddha Sahitya Sabha, 1950.

———. *The Early Buddhist Theory of Man Perfected.* London : Williams and Norgate, 1936.

Jacobi, Herman, ed. and tr. *Jaina Sūtras.* Sacred Books of the East. Vol. 25; reprint ed., Delhi : Motilal Banarsidass, 1968.

Jayatilleke, K. N. *The Message of the Buddha.* Edited by Ninian Smart. New York : The Free Press, 1975.

Kalupahana, David. *Buddhist Philosophy : a Historical Analysis.* Honolulu : University of Hawaii Press, 1976.

Kern, H. Manual of Indian Buddhism. Reprint ed., Varanasi : Indological Book House, 1968; originally published in Strassburg, 1896.

Kitagawa, Joseph M. *Religions of the East.* Philadelphia : The Westminster Press, 1958.

La Vallée Poussin, Louis de. *The Buddhist Councils.* Calcutta : K. P. Bagchi & Company, 1976; originally published as an article, "The Buddhist Councils." *Indian Antiquary* 37 (1908) : 1-18, 81-106.

———. *The Way to Nirvāṇa.* Cambridge, U. K. : Cambridge University Press, 1917.

———. *La Morale Buddhique.* Paris : Nouvelle Libraire Nationale, 1927.

Laeuchli, Samuel. *Power and Sexuality : The Emergence of Canon Law at the Synod of Elvira.* Philadelphia : Temple University Press, 1972.

Law, B. C. "The Concept of Morality in Buddhism and Jainism." *Journal of the Bombay Branch of the Royal Asiatic Society* 34-35 (1959-60) : 1-21.

———. *A History of Pāli Literature.* 2 vols. London : Oxford University Press, 1933.

Levi, Sylvain. "Sur la recitation primitive textes bouddhique." *Journal Asiatique* (1915) : 401-47.

Luk, Charles, ed. and tr. *The Vimilakirti Nirdesa Sutra.* Berkeley : Shambhala Publications, 1976.

Misra, G. S. P. *The Age of Vinaya.* New Delhi : Munshiram Manoharlal, 1972.

Murti, T. R. V. *The Central Philosophy of Buddhism.* London : George Allen and Unwin, Ltd., 1955.

Nagai, N. "Buddhist *Vinaya* Discipline or Buddhist Commandments." In *Buddhistic Studies*. Edited by B. C. Law. Calcutta : Thacker, Spink and Company, 1931, pp. 365-82.

Ñāṇamoli Thera, tr. *The Pāṭimokkha*. Bangkok : The Social Science Association of Thailand, 1966.

Obeyesekere, Gananath; Reynolds, Frank; and Smith, Bardwell. *The Two Wheels of Dhamma : Essays on the Theravada Tradition in India and Ceylon*. American Academy of Religion Studies in Religion No. 3. Chambersburg, Pa. : The American Academy of Religion, 1972.

Oldenberg, Hermann. *The Buddha : His Life, His Doctrine, His Order*. Translated by William Hoey. London : Williams and Norgate, 1882.

Pachow, W. "Legal Dealings Between the Buddhist Saṃgha and the Laity." *Proceedings and Transactions of the All-India Oriental Conference* (October, 1946) : pp. 349-55.

———. *A Comparative Study of the Prātimokṣa Sūtra*. Santiniketan, India : Sino-Indian Cultural Society, 1955.

Pande, Govind C. *Studies in the Origins of Buddhism*. Allahabad: University Department of Ancient History, Culture and Archeology, 1957.

Prebish, Charles S. *Buddhist Monastic Discipline : The Sanskrit Prātimokṣa Sūtras of the Mahāsāṃghikas and Mūlasarvāstivādins*. University Park, Pa. : The Pennsylvania State University Press, 1975.

———. "The Prātimokṣa Puzzle : Fact versus Fantasy." *Journal of the American Oriental Society* 94 (April 1974) : 168-76.

———. "A Review of Scholarship on the Buddhist Councils." *Journal of Asian Studies* 33 (February 1974) : 239-54.

———. "Theories Concerning the Skandhaka : An Appraisal." *Journal of Asian Studies* 32 (August, 1973) : 669-78.

Prebish, Charles S., and Nattier, Janice J. "Mahāsāṃghika Origins : The Beginnings of Buddhist Sectarianism." *History of Religions* 16 (February 1977) : 237-72.

Przyluski, Jean. *Le concile de Rājagṛha*. Paris : Paul Geuthner, 1926-28.

Rahula, Walpola. *What the Buddha Taught*. Foreword by Paul Demieville. 2nd Edition. New York : Grove Press, 1974.

Reynolds, Frank. "The Several Bodies of Buddha : Reflections on a Neglected Aspect of Theravada Tradition." *History of Religions* 16 (May, 1977).

Robertson, Alec. *The Triple Gem and the Uposatha*. Colombo : The Colombo Apothecaries Company, Ltd., 1971.

Saddhatissa, H. *Buddhist Ethics*. London : George Allen and Unwin, Ltd., 1970.

———. *The Life of the Buddha*. New York : Harper and Row, Publishers, 1976.

Sarkisyanz, Emmanuel. *The Buddhist Backgrounds of the Burmese Revolution*. The Hague : Martinus Nijhoff, 1965.

Sasaki, George H. "The Concept of Kamma in Buddhist Philosophy." *Oriens Extremus* 3 (1956) : 185-204.

Shastri, Ajay M. *An Outline of Early Buddhism*. Varanasi : Indological Book House, 1965.

Stcherbatsky, Fedor I. *Buddhist Logic*. 2 vols. Leningrad : Academy of Sciences of the USSR, 1930-32; reprint ed., The Hague : Mouton and Co., 1958.

Tachibana, S. *The Ethics of Buddhism*. London : Oxford University Press, 1926; reprint ed., New York : Harper and Row, Publishers, 1975.

Takakusu, Junjirō. *The Essentials of Buddhist Philosophy*. Edited by Wing-tsit Chan and Charles A. Moore. Honolulu : Office Appliance Co., 1956; reprint ed. Westport, Conn. : Greenwood Press, 1973.

Tambiah, Stanley J. *Buddhism and the Spirit Cults in North-east Thailand*. Cambridge, U. K. : Cambridge University Press, 1970.

Thomas, Edward J. *Early Buddhist Scriptures*. London : Kegan Paul, Trench, Trübner, and Co., 1935.

———. *The History of Buddhist Thought*. London : Kegan Paul, Trench, Trübner, and Co., 1933.

———. *Life of Buddha as Legend and History*. 3rd ed. London : Routledge and Kegan Paul, 1949.

van Buitenen, J. A. B. "Vedic and Upaniṣadic Bases of Indian Civilization." In *Chapters in Indian Civilization*. Edited by Joseph Elder. 4 vols. Dubuque, Ia: Kendall/Hall Publishing Co., 1970. 1:1-38.

Varma, Vishwanath P. *Early Buddhism and Its Origins.* New Delhi : Munshiram Manoharlal, 1973.

———. "The Origins and Sociology of the Early Buddhist Philosophy of Moral Determinism." *Philosophy East and West* 13 (April, 1963) : 25-48.

Wach, Joachim. *The Comparative Study of Religion.* Edited with an Introduction by Joseph M. Kitagawa. New York : Columbia University Press, 1958.

Warder, Anthony K. *Indian Buddhism.* Delhi : Motilal Banarsidass, 1970.

Wijesekera, O. H. de A. *Knowledge and Conduct : Buddhist Philosophy and Ethics.* The Wheel Publication No. 50. Kandy : Buddhist Publication Society, 1963.

Winternitz, Maurice. *History of Indian Literature.* Translated by S. Ketkar. 2 vols. Calcutta : Calcutta University Press, 1927, 1932.

INDEX